Free Tickets

Free Tickets

How One Man Changed the Cultural Life of a Community

With best wishes
Helen Mosby

Helen Clopton Polk Mosby

Audience Press

LIBRARY OF CONGRESS CATALOGING-IN-PUBLICATION DATA
Mosby, Helen Clopton Polk, 1909-
Free tickets : how one man changed the cultural life of a
community / Helen Clopton Polk Mosby.
    p.   cm.
ISBN 0-87483-557-7 (pbk. : alk. paper)
1. Concerts—Arkansas—Helena.   2. Music—Arkansas—
Helena—History and criticism. 3. Warfield, Samuel Drake.
I. Title.
ML200.8.H45M67   1999
780'.78'.76788—dc21   98-49233

To my first husband,

Cadwallader Leonidas Polk Jr.

who had he lived would
have enjoyed Warfield Concerts
more than anyone in the world.

Samuel Drake Warfield

Who more than anyone
took us in mind and spirit far from Helena
to that world at large a knowledge of which
makes us all the more fondly aware
of whence we come.

—George E. Nolthenius de Man
from HELENA: THE RIDGE, THE RIVER, THE ROMANCE

Contents

Introduction

Today is January 1, 1992, one of those cold, crystal clear days, which fills one with energy, ambition, and hope. It is a perfect day for the football games—the Rose Bowl, Cotton Bowl, Sugar Bowl, Orange Bowl, and all the other newborn bowls that take place on New Year's day. Game parties will serve black-eyed peas and hog jowl, southern food that is considered to bring good fortune to those who partake of it on the first day of the year.

It is the day for making New Year's resolutions. Some will vow to "turn over a new leaf" by resolving to improve their lives or to correct bad habits. Of course, as a rule, most of these good intentions will be soon forgotten, leaving only those with firm self-discipline and an iron will to carry out their promises.

As for me, now in my eighty-second year, I no longer make plans for the future. Life has become a game of thankfulness as I open my eyes each morning and find myself still here. Like the antique clock on the mantel that has kept time for three generations, I continue to tick. Instead of looking forward, I choose to think back over the years. Some things that seemed rather bad at the time turned out to have been for the best. My Easter dress that I made at age fourteen was a failure, but it was also the beginning of years of useful sewing. I realize how friends and events have influenced my life. Even little remarks my mother and father used to make left a lasting impression on me. Whether it was an admonition to brush my teeth or an injunction to greet all chaperons at parties and dances, these and other parental words of wisdom that I received during my youth have not been forgotten. Indeed, these memories and others have become increasingly more vivid in the final years of my long, eventful life.

Reflecting on bygone days makes me appreciate more than ever my work on the Warfield Concerts Committee. I received unique satisfaction when working with professional musicians and their management companies, entertaining artists, planning programs and publicity, pleasing the public, and working with fellow Warfield committee members. It was hard work, but I have enjoyed every minute.

On this very day twenty-five years ago, Samuel Drake Warfield died from a sudden heart attack. His quick, unexpected death was a shock that filled my husband Winston and me with sadness; both of us considered S.D. to be a true and dear friend. Naturally, we wondered what would happen to his estate when he died, since D. was a bachelor with no immediate family. However, the answer to that question came when his bequest was made known to the public of Helena, Arkansas. That will changed the face of our proud little town of 10,000 people that is situated on the west bank of the mighty Mississippi.

Such memories of S.D. and his extraordinary gift must never be forgotten. Therefore, on this cold, clear day, I too make a New Year's resolution: I hereby resolve in this year of our Lord, one thousand nine-hundred ninety-two, to recount "The Warfield Story," so that future generations will never forget SD's generous and gracious gift.

—Helen Clopton Polk Mosby

S.D.

Although Samuel Drake Warfield had a most distinguished name, he was always known as S.D. or to intimate friends just plain D. To call young boys by their initials, rather than by their full names was frequent in the Mississippi Delta area, particularly in the early part of the twentieth century.

S.D. came into the world on November 29, 1900. His parents were Fanny and Sam Warfield and had been married quite some time before he was born. They first lived on Ohio Street, then an elite residential area, which ran north and south, parallel to the river.

The homes were, for the most part, white frame homes with gingerbread trim and wrap round porches. All of these houses faced the levee and were built high off the ground because of the problem of flooding. Ohio Street was often under water when the river rose, so much so that in some places a light boat could be used to move about. Oftentimes, water levels swelled to the danger point, especially if spring rains had been heavy and when melted snow and ice washed down from the north. Not until the thirties and the arrival of the United States Engineers did Old Man River begin to be controlled.

I can remember the ice jam of 1939 when huge blocks of ice decided to float down the river unmelted. They formed a solid surface right at Helena. One lone man decided to walk across the frozen river. He did it successfully and unharmed, but no one has ever tried that before or since. On that occasion, Helena made the news in a big way—including pictures in *Life*.

The Warfields spent happy days on Ohio Street, sharing neighborly customs, conversations, food, music, and entertainment with the Coolidge and Barlow families. Watermelon parties, candy pulls, and singing romantic ballads around the piano were part of the fun. Mary Elizabeth Coolidge kept the singing going with her beautiful high soprano. These families remained life-long friends even when the Warfields moved into a modest two-story red brick home that they built on Porter Street. The house was located across the street from what is now the First Presbyterian Church and next door to the nineteenth century house used today by the Gladin family for a home and photographic studio. During these times, S.D. was a very young man.

Mr. and Mrs. Warfield and D. were devoted members of the First United Methodist Church of Helena, and for the greater part of his life, S.D. acted as the treasurer of the Sunday School Department. As a memorial to his father and mother, he gave tasteful, well-chosen furnishings to the beautiful little chapel, which adjoined the church. He also had a part in choosing the restful blue of the interior.

His father died first, a big loss for a small family of three. S.D. and his mother continued to live in the red brick. Mrs. Warfield was a lady of the Old South and an active member of the U.D.C. (United Daughters of the Confederacy). She and her dear friends, Mrs. Coolidge and Mrs. Fannie Mae Hornor, were Southern patriots. Until their dying days, they made regular visits to the Confederate Veterans Cemetery on the top peak of Maple Hill.

I wish they could know how well this hallowed spot has been nurtured in recent years. The wrought-iron fence and benches are freshly painted, monuments have been cleaned, and new plantings of shrubs and flowers have made this hilltop spot a place of beauty that touches the soul.

Fanny Warfield died about 1933, but not before she had instilled the importance of being a southern gentleman in her son. He was all that and more. The "and more" refers to the touch of the titled Englishman in some of his mannerisms, ornamented with a few *bon mots* which he delighted in portraying on special occasions. He tipped his hat, bowed, and in exalted moods would bend and kiss a lady's hand by way of greeting.

This Warfield son became a young bachelor with no immediate family. He was well-dressed, and a lean five feet eleven inches—including hat and coat. He always wore a white shirt, tie, and brightly polished shoes. In summer, he wore a white linen suit and a panama hat. He knew the correct outfit to wear for any occasion and was most fastidious about his clothes. When buying a new suit, he demanded the entire attention of the sales staff of Ciener's Mens Store, Helena's highly regarded haberdashery. And, almost without exception, he relied on the advice and expertise of his longtime friend, Tom Short, head salesman, to coordinate the details of each outfit.

He was only a spectator sports fan—except for frequent indulgement in dancing, if dancing can be called a sport. He knew all the latest steps as well as the old-fashioned waltz, foxtrot, and tango. The ladies, both young and old, loved to dance with D. So well did he perform this social sport that we called him the "Helena Fred Astaire." Indeed, he did have a slight resemblance to the world famous Astaire, and nothing pleased him more than to be compared to that toe-tapping man. He glowed with compliments such as "S.D., I declare you remind me so much of Fred Astaire" or "Hey D, that's my favorite waltz. Let's trip the light fantastic."

The Duke and Duchess of Windsor, the abdicated Edward and his American wife, Wallie, shared the top spot on his celebrity list. He felt there was a family connection with Wallie since one of her names was Warfield. In fact, he actually professed to be related to her. He was extremely proud of this fact and made it a point to keep up with their lives, vicariously enjoying all that they did.

He liked to talk at great length about royalty. In the late twenties, D. and his friend, Leland Stone, went to Europe—the one and only time that S.D. ever left the United States. He forever after used this soul exposure to foreign territory as a base for all conversations pertaining to England and her aristocracy or to any of the other European nobility.

In December 1942, during World War II, our Polk family was stationed in Miami Beach, Florida, with the Army Air Force, where my first husband, Cad Polk, was the Provost Marshall. One of his duties was to provide security for the visiting VIPs. It so happened that the Duke and Duchess arrived on the beach for a day of Christmas shopping. The exclusive gift shops on Lincoln Road locked the doors when these celebrities were inside in order to assure complete and safe privacy. I was green with envy that Cad could be with them all day while I was limited to an occasional glimpse from the street. As the day moved along, Edward requested a bar in spite of protests from Wallie. Since the Duke's authority was respected, off to the bar they went. With polite tact, Cad asked the Duke to autograph the bar card, which he graciously did. This famous autograph we mailed to D, who sounded such joy, such exclamations of delight, over what he considered a priceless possession.

He did not have any formal education beyond high school or any desire to attend college. Dormitories, rigid schedules, and torment endured by freshmen college students in the 1910s were things completely foreign to his personality. Rather, S.D. acquired an amazing amount of knowledge from perusing the newspapers and from conversations with friends. He could converse intelligently on nearly any subject and always had respect for the proper use of English grammar.

However, S.D. did adopt a college, the University of Mississippi. He was impressed by the Confederate flags and southern atmosphere that prevailed there and was as loyal and supportive as any alumnus that was ever graduated by Ole Miss. He loved the Rebels; when they won a game, he was in ecstasy, and when they lost, he grieved. Whatever the result, when the game was over and a post game party took place, he was ready to join the crowd, conversing profusely with each and everyone there and indulging with delight in good food and drink.

In contrast to his love of sports, opera and classical music were another of his passions. In the days of the Civic Music Association, D. was one of the first people to buy a ticket and attend every concert. In fact, he served on the fund-raising committee. He knew not one note from another, but his depth of appreciation for classical music was unlimited. For example, attending the opera season in Memphis was a highlight of the year. The magnificent Metropolitan Opera Company made a three-day stop in Memphis each year on their Spring Tour, which brought to the Mid-South the elegance of grand opera. D, dressed to perfection in his evening clothes, was always euphoric to check in at the Peabody Hotel and attend all three performances. Oftentimes a friend would be invited to go with him, but the friend had to be properly attired for the occasion.

One reason why D. was happy to stay at the Peabody was because the entire Met cast stayed there. After the performance, if fate chose to be kind to D, there was a chance for a cordial nod or even a brief conversation. His ultimate experience was when he showered a famous diva with words of praise and admiration backstage, after the curtain closed. D. never forgot that encounter and always remembered her sparkling high C.

He and I often discussed opera. Opera offered everything, we both agreed; the staging, the drama and plot, together with sensational voices were part of this stupendous production.

People have frequently asked both during and after his life: "Where does Samuel Drake Warfield get his money? What does he live on? He has a home, a nice car, many fine clothes—almost anything he needs. How does he do it?"

The answers lie in the following. D's parents left him several small farms in Phillips and Lee counties, and the rent from them was enough for one person to have a good living without having to worry over finances. Although he had no part in the actual operation of his farms, he felt that it was his duty to suffer until the farming season was over. It was as if his occupation in life was to worry and sympathize with the people who rented from him. Bad weather was a plague. It was either too dry or too much rain, and the looming threat of boll weevils or Johnson grass taking over concerned him deeply. His daily anguish over the crop took place during the morning coffee break around the table of friends at the Post Office Cafe, where D. had breakfasted earlier. His first visit of the day was a ritualistic 6:30 A.M. repast with two cups of coffee. After scrutinizing the *Commercial Appeal* from cover to cover, he took himself for a ride round town to assess the weather conditions for farming. Then he'd head back home to rest awhile until it was time to revisit the restaurant for more coffee and news.

When D. had no dinner invitation or other pressing engagement, he could be found again in the late afternoon at the Post Office Cafe, which we called the P.O. It was owned for many years by Mr. George Andrews. If this modest little P.O. had ears and could talk, what tales would be told; stories of gossip and scandal, news of that day, business transactions, romance, and arguments that took place there would fill volumes.

When D. wasn't worrying or conversing at the P.O., his interest in the arts, culture, and social graces absorbed his time. He shared his artistic interests with his many friends, and by most people, he was called a gentleman of leisure.

For one with no immediate family, S.D. Warfield had more family connections than anyone I ever knew. His friends were his family. He shared in their family life and the activities of their children. He considered weddings a great event. I would wager that he broke the record for the number of times he had been a groomsman. I remember that after he was in the wedding of Frances and Allen Keesee, he asked them to use the upstairs of the Warfield home for living quarters—which they did, during their early years of their marriage.

Almost daily, he was in touch with Josephine and Francis Thompson in the big Victorian house on Perry Street, and he watched their son, George de Man, grow up and go to Harvard. When George married in Atlanta, Georgia, D. had a big weekend of wedding festivities in this large southern city. The nearness of Stone Mountain memorial to the Confederacy was a temptation he could not resist. Leaving his partying crowd for a short while, our southern gentleman drove himself to the mountain to gaze in awe at his favorites, Robert E. Lee, Stonewall Jackson, and Jefferson Davis.

Social life was ever present in the Thompson home, and S.D. was part of it. Dinner at eight when we "dressed" was the epitome of elegance. Josephine presided at the head of the long table that was covered with Irish linens while we dined in style from soup to nuts. Our Warfield benefactor relished every bite and reveled in the spicy conversation.

In Frank A. Jeffett's book, *This Love of Hunting*, he tells of a party with D: "I remember one night just after we were home from the army. We were all in Memphis, dancing away the night, having a delightful evening, and on the way back to Helena about 5:00 A.M. D. began reciting 'my candle burns at both ends. It may not last the night. But ah my friends and oh my foes, it makes a lovely light.'" I think the spirit of the poem showed his love for life and his great enthusiasm and zest for living as well as his completely loyal friendship and devotion to his good friends.

In my own household, he joined us for supper once or twice a week. He had a great taste for freshly cooked vegetables and used to say, "I never apologize for eating an onion. It's very bourgeois." In contrast, Winston wanted only bread, meat, and potatoes, while D. and I had a feast on a variety of freshly cooked vitamin-filled produce.

At Christmas time, everyone was remembered. D. liked to send flowers, but the order was not given on the telephone. He went to the florist shop and personally selected each fresh blossom used in the arrangement. His bouquets were truly lovely. Even now I bring out at Christmas time one of the big fancy red candles he gave us for a centerpiece. He did not ever lack for invitations to Christmas dinner from the numerous families that claimed him as one of them. We all loved him, and when this kind generous man left the world there were many sad hearts.

That Last Day

On January 2, 1967, when I came into my house after an early morning visit to Kroger's Supermarket for urgently need groceries, I heard Leola, my trusted maid of 19 years, say, "Mrs. Mosby, a call came, Mr. Warfield has passed."

"Leola, who are you talking about?" I replied. "Surely not Mr. S.D. Warfield. Why that can't be true. He was out last night at a party. And besides, he has never been ill in his life."

I called Josephine Thompson, one of S.D.'s dearest friends who always knew his whereabouts, to see what she might know, but the answer was the same. Samuel Drake Warfield was dead. Our southern gentleman with his *joie de vivre* was gone forever.

His last day on earth, that fatal January 1, 1967, could only be called a glorious one. If someone had told him to plan his last hours, I think his choice would have been exactly what he actually did. The weather was perfect. In the morning, spirits were high in anticipation over the big bowl games. Butterflies fluttered inside, and hands were icy cold. Who would win these terrific football contests?

Fortunately the Sun Bowl, played at El Paso, Texas, on December 30th, was over. The participating teams were the University of Texas and the University of Mississippi. Coach John Vaught's Ole Miss Rebels fought valiantly and lost.

S.D. had managed to recover from the agony and humiliation of the defeat of his beloved Ole Miss and had returned to his usual football exuberance.

Together with friends, D. watched the games. A TV party it was called. With pride he cheered; he clapped and shouted. Each passing minute his enthusiasm rose as he saw his favorites winning. "Oh my! It's over and we've won!" he exclaimed. "What a sensational experience. A celebration is in order."

Well, with perfect timing, he gave a little dinner party. Where? The Country Club was closed after the big New Year's Eve dance. So he took his guests to the Holiday Inn. Included in the party were George de Man and his wife Andrea and Dr. Aris and Julianne Cox.

They drank champagne, laughed and talked, and ate T-bone steaks. But by 10:00 P.M., bodies ran low on adrenaline, and it was good-night.

At home again, D. settled himself in. His house was comfortable with three bedrooms upstairs, but for S.D. his bedroom was in the parlor downstairs, and his bed was the big sofa amid a mound of newspapers. He always slept there.

According to Dr. Macon Kirkman, the call came just before midnight. "Come quickly, Oh please, I'm in such terrible pain," said the strained voice on the other end of the line. Dr. Kirkman, only a few blocks away, was there in no time. S.D. had managed to unlock the front door, but he was dying. A very few minutes and he was gone. Dr. Kirkman later remarked to his friends, "Had D. been willing to have regular physical examinations with perhaps some medication, I feel he would have lived another ten years, but he had a perfect horror of a doctor's office. I'm dreadfully sorry that he would not take care of himself."

His funeral took place on January 3, 1967. Here is the newspaper report as written in the *East Arkansas Record*:

WARFIELD SERVICES ARE HELD HERE THIS AFTERNOON

Mr. S.D. Warfield, a prominent and well-known Helena resident since his birth at the turn of the century, succumbed at his home on Porter Street at 1 o'clock Monday morning as the result of a heart attack.

Mr. Warfield was a holder of numerous farming interests in Lee and Phillips Counties and was a member of the St. Francis Levee Board for many years. He was an active and faithful member of the First Methodist church here and was known for his thoughtful generosity in connection with all local charities.

He is survived by his aunt, Mrs. C.M. Warfield of Lexa, and his cousins, Mrs. R.L. Sayle, Mr. R.P. Gist, Mr. Warfield Gist, Mr. C.C. Warfield, Mrs. Raymond

Holder of Helena and Mr. Robert M. Wilkes of Austin, Texas.

Pallbearers for the service held at the First Methodist Church at 2 o'clock this afternoon were Francis Thompson, A.R. Keesee, Jim Pillow, Frank Jeffett, Adolph Feldman, Winston Mosby, Morse Gist, Bobby Hornor and Stuart Orr.

The family has asked that in accordance with the wish of the deceased, memorials be made to the First Methodist Church and the Ophelia Polk Moore Orphans Home.

Interment was in Maple Hill Cemetery with Citizens Funeral Home in charge.

Four Years Later

My calendar at this very minute reads January 1, 1996. The time is 10 P.M., and I am holding a pen in my hand.

Earlier in the evening, a few old friends gathered here to wish each other a Happy New Year. Among them were Teedie Anders, Meriam Solomon, Katie Miller, Doc Baker, Myron Schrantz, and Charles Conditt. I refer to them informally because they will be more fully identified in a later chapter of this book.

We sat around the fire, reminisced about "the good old days," and enjoyed a bit of wine, cheese, some snacks, and my chocolate angel food cake. The same stories had been shared time and time again, but always we listened with smiles and laughter.

We remembered Delta Sigma (high school fraternity) dances in blazing summer weather, when the only half-way cool air came from electric fans blowing on huge blocks of ice, riding around in rumble seats of old cars to keep cool in ninety degree weather and putting hot bricks in those same cars to warm up in winter, fixing flat tires that would not stay pumped up,

Doc dressing as Robin Hood for a fancy dress party, and Helen singing a solo, graduation 1927.

We liked to talk about the experiences that occurred during World War II. At that time, Myron and Janet, after only three week's acquaintance, married just a few months before he was sent overseas and Winston spent five years in what he called a foot-walking infantry, fought in the trenches in France, and hitch-hiked home from Seattle, Washington, when the war ended. Doc entered the service as a private and rose to the rank of major. He was also in Paris on V-E (Victory in Europe) Day, May 7, 1945 and in Tokyo Bay on V-J Day. The conversation went on and on.

Eight-thirty on this New Year celebration of 1996 came all too soon, but there was Louis at the back door to drive everyone home. Four years had passed since I have written a single word on the Warfield story.

How could four years pass without adding a single word? There are, however, a few acceptable excuses. In the spring of 1992, I had cataract surgery with complications which, two months later, required more surgery. When that was over, another cataract was removed. Housekeeping had escalated as Clopton and Polky became teenagers. My daughter Libby is their mother, and all three live with me. Summers in Monteagle, Tennessee, where I concentrate on water-color painting, attend programs and concerts offered by the Monteagle Assembly, and indulge in a little social life, certainly gave no encouragement to the solitary world of writing a book.

Without realizing it, I allowed myself to be weaned from this project. My thoughts were moving in other directions except for an occasional prick of conscience that said, "Don't forget S.D." I have not forgotten, and I want to renew the New year's resolution I made exactly four years ago to write the Warfield Story.

The Famous Will

Why did S.D. make such a will? Why did he not leave his money to his relatives or good friends? What was his inspiration? Who wrote the will?

I have asked myself these questions. I have also discussed these questions with S.D.'s very loyal and intimate friends who loved him dearly and most deeply appreciated his unique gift. We all fully agree and feel that it is correct to say that he was initially inspired by his interest in the local Civic Music Association now known as Community Concerts.

Helena has had the distinction of being the smallest town in the United States that was ever a part of the Civic Music Association. A small group of hard-working music lovers sold tickets each year to give our town the musical refinement and culture that the concerts provided. The drive to sell season tickets lasted one week. Through the supreme effort of Mrs. Seelig Mundt, affectionately called Miss Josie, success was achieved. Miss Josie was a great musician herself. A pianist and splendid vocal accompanist, her world was classical music. She truly believed she did someone a favor when she convinced him or her to buy a ticket. Her gentle persuasive manner sold many tickets. Through her influence, Helena became a Civic Music Community. She worked untiringly to get it started and remained loyal to the cause throughout her life.

How well I remember the parties she gave after the concerts. She entertained the artists, who were usually given a complete meal (most musicians do not eat a heavy dinner before a performance) in the kitchen area, while others enjoyed refreshments in the dining room, including her specialty, homemade cake. Gorgeous cakes they were, chocolate cake, white cake, lemon cake, and fruit cake to name a few. I can still almost taste that rich chocolate icing.

At first, the Civic Music performances took place in the opera house on the corner of Walnut and Porter Streets—until it burned. Other places used were Temple Bethel, the auditorium at the old Helena High School, and even sometimes the Twentieth Century Club. Miss Josie kept things going.

Built in 1870, the opera house was one of the three finest in the South, designed with boxes and a dress circle like the old European *theatres*. Of course there were also two balconies and an orchestra pit. Helena was on the circuit for such traveling productions as *Maggie and Jiggs, A.G. Fields Minstrels, Blossom Time*, and *The Merry Widow*. Among the successful amateur productions was *Carmen*, starring Nina Heden (later Mrs. Ervin Beisel) and directed by Kurth

Donath of the famous Donath School of Music. Mr.
Donath also directed the Melody Club, which gave
annual concerts at our opera house. How sad to lose
such a jewel.

Those Civic Music Concerts then must surely have
been the inspiration that developed into Warfield
Concerts. Those concerts inspired S.D. Warfield to
write his astonishing will in November 1939—the
contents of which were never revealed until after his
death. He probably also knew from experience how
hard the Civic Music tickets were to sell. "Well, I'll fix
that," he thought, "and leave my estate so that all the
concerts will be free. No more tickets to sell!"

An exhibit of the complete will with all its legal
terms and signatures can be found in the back of this
book. As can be seen, the will was signed on
November 6, 1939 and was witnessed by W.R. Orr and
Thomas M. Short, both of whom were S.D.'s intimate
lifelong friends. S.D. lived 28 more years after the
signing of this document, but during all that time there
were no amendments.

It always amazes me when I think back through the
'70s, the '80s, and now into the '90s and realize how
well the provisions therein have worked out. I think
S.D. would be extremely pleased with the way his
bequest has been used. In his wildest dreams he could
not have imagined that he would receive recognition
all over the United States. Warfield Concerts has
become one of the finest concert series in the country.

The Warfield Committee is in constant communication with booking agents everywhere. Their salesmen are continually surprised to learn that the concerts are free and that performing artists who come to Helena say it is a compliment to be part of the series. Reporters and journalists have been here for information, and stories have been in the *New York Times, Southern Living Magazine, Musical America, Atlanta Journal,* and numerous other publications.

One reporter I remember well was Diane Goldsmith from the *Atlanta Journal.* She spent three days here. After gathering all the information she wanted about Warfield Concerts, she became so interested in the historical aspect of Helena, plus meeting Miss Lily Peter, that she stayed. The result was a full page write-up in the *Journal.*

Another of S.D.'s good friends was former Helenian Frank A. Jeffett, who wrote *This Love of Hunting,* wherein he devoted a whole chapter to S.D. With Mr. Jeffett's permission, I quote a few thoughts from it concerning "The Will." "It is a most unusual will that would benefit all the residents of the Helena area, and indeed, I think it will come to benefit everyone from the Mid-South especially many people in the Delta who are interested in music.

S.D.'s first interest in life was his good friends. Along with that, he was a devoted churchman to both the Helena Methodist Church, where he was a member, and to St. John's Episcopal Church, where we often went to church together. He said that if he ever left Helena, he would join the Episcopal Church in a moment, but having grown up in the Methodist Church, he felt a real loyalty and devotion and would never change his membership. (When you read the will, you will see he left $500 to each church).

In addition to his close friends and his church, S.D. had a great love of music that was most clearly disclosed in his will, which provided for the bulk of his estate to be placed in the Warfield Foundation Trust to be created at his death for the purpose of funding free concerts. The will spelled out that a committee be appointed in the city of Helena to hold free annual concerts for the benefit of all people.

S.D. was a great friend, a true and loyal friend that not many people are privileged to have—a fine gentleman, full of zest, and a generous benefactor to all through the Warfield Foundation. He had a keen wit, was an ardent conversationalist, and was a generous host who loved to entertain his friends for cocktails and dinner. S.D. was our true and selfless friend who is now gone, but whose memory will linger on always with those of us who were his closest friends. He has left in perpetuity to the citizens of the Mid-South and particularly those in Helena and Phillips County a legacy that is second to none and is unparalleled in the world of music. S.D. made this available to thousands who will enjoy his gift in the years to come.

WILL OF S.D. WARFIELD

I, S.D. Warfield, of Helena, Phillips County, Arkansas, being over the age of twenty-one years and of sound and disposing mind and memory, do hereby make, publish and declare this to be my last will and testament, hereby revoking all wills heretofore made by me at any time.

ARTICLE I: I direct that all my just debts be paid as speedily as possible.

ARTICLE II: I give and bequeath the following legacies to be paid out of or given from my estate after the payment of my debts.

(1) To my cousin, Robert Wilkes, of Helena, Arkansas, the sum of Twenty-Five Hundred Dollars ($2500.00).

(2) To my aunt, Mrs. Wilbur Gresham, of Madison, Georgia, or her heirs, the sum of One Thousand Dollars ($1000.00).

(3) To my cousin, Mrs. D.S. Wagnon, of Macon, Georgia, or her heirs, the jewelry, china and other personal effects which I inherited from my mother, Mrs. Fannie T. Warfield.

(4) To the Board of Deacons of the Methodist Episcopal Church, of Helena, Arkansas the sum of Five Hundred Dollars ($500.00) to be used in the erection of memorial doors and door lamps in memory of my father, Samuel Drake Warfield, unless, in the discretion of said Board of Deacons, suitable doors and lamps shall have been erected between the time of the writing of this will and the date that it shall become effective;

in the event that they feel the same have been so erected, then said sum to be used in the erection of such other permanent memorial as they may deem suitable which has the approval of my executor.

(5) To the Rectors, Wardens and Vestry of St. John's Episcopal Church, the sum of Five Hundred Dollars ($500.00) to be used in their discretion in the erection in that church of a permanent memorial which has the approval of my executor.

ARTICLE III: I devise and bequeath all the rest and residue of my estate, real, personal and mixed, unto my trustee, hereinafter named and designated, to have and to hold the same upon the trust hereinafter set forth.

ARTICLE IV: I appoint the Union National Bank of Little Rock, Arkansas, to be my trustee under this my will. It is understood and agreed that any corporation or association which by reason of any merger, consolidation or transfer of assets may succeed to all, or substantially all, of the business of the trustee, automatically, and without the execution or filing of any instrument, or any further act, deed or conveyance on the part of any of the parties hereto, shall be and become the successor of the trustee hereunder and vested with all of the title to the trust funds and it, as well as any other successor trustee hereunder, shall possess all the powers, discretions, immunities, and privileges as did the above named Union National Bank as the original trustee hereunder.

ARTICLE V: I authorize my trustee to retain, without liability for loss or depreciation resulting from such retention, original property, real or personal, at any time received by it from the executor for such time as to it shall seem best, although such property may not be of the character prescribed by law or by the terms of this instrument for the investment of other trust funds and although it represents a large percentage of the total property of the trust estate; and to dispose of such original property by sale or exchange or otherwise as and when it shall deem advisable and receive and administer proceeds as a part of the trust estate. My trustee is authorized to invest and reinvest the trust funds from time to time, without restrictions as to the kind or character of property in which such investments shall be made, and regardless as to whether or not such investments are those specifically authorized for trustees under the statute laws of the State of Arkansas or of any other states to which the administration of my estate may be subject; and my trustee shall not be liable for any loss in any investment made by it except in cases where it would have been liable had the investment been one authorized by statute.

(1) My trustee shall stand possessed of said rest and residue of my estate, to be known as the WARFIELD FOUNDATION, for the following purpose: to pay three per cent (3%) of the value of said rest and residue of my estate as it is appraised annually on the anniversary of my death to a committee to be constituted as hereinafter provided, the value of said rest and residue of my estate to be determined for the purpose of such annual appraisal by adding all the income accumulated at that date to the principal of the trust; the amount so paid to be disbursed by that committee to provide an annual musical concert or concerts to be known as the WARFIELD FOUNDATION CONCERTS; said concerts to be held in Helena, Arkansas and free to the inhabitants of that city regardless of race, creed or color.

(2) The committee to sponsor said concerts shall be residents of Helena, Arkansas and selected as follows: one each by the Protestant Episcopal Minister and the Jewish Rabbi serving the people of Helena, and the Third by the Mayor or chief executive officers of the City of Helena; a majority of said committee is to have absolute discretion, within the terms of this trust, in providing said concerts; the expenses of this committee shall be paid out of the proceeds of the Foundation, but the members shall serve without compensation.

(3) The committee shall keep records of their proceedings, receipts and disbursements, a copy of which shall be filed with the trustee on or before the 15th day of January of each year. The receipts and disbursements of the committee as well as of the trustee shall be published annually in the newspaper published in the City of Helena reputed to have the largest circulation therein. Failure to make such publication shall authorize any court of competent jurisdiction to appoint another trustee in the event the court shall find that neglect to make such publication is due to gross negligence of the trustee. Either the Attorney General of the State of Arkansas or the law officer of the City of Helena shall have the right to institute appropriate proceedings to insure the proper administration of this trust.

(4) My trustee shall be entitled to reasonable compensation for its services; the reasonableness thereof is always to be subject to review by the Chancery Court of Phillips County, Arkansas, in proceedings which may be instituted by either the Attorney General of the State of Arkansas or the law officer of the City of Helena.

(5) It is my intention herein to honor my father, Samuel Drake Warfield, and my mother, Fannie Tuggle

Warfield, by the _____ of my _____ _____ by the establishing of a perpetual charitable trust, to promote the education and aesthetic enjoyment of the community in which this estate has been accumulated.

ARTICLE VI: My trustee is authorized to elect which portions of my residuary estate, real, personal and mixed, it may not care to accept as part of the trust estate. Such portions as it may not care to accept shall be converted by my executor, as soon as practicable, into cash or securities which will be acceptable by my trustee, and the net income therefrom added to the trust estate. I authorize and empower my executor, and any successor, to sell and dispose of such portions of my estate as my trustee may designate for conversion into cash or securities as hereinabove set out, either at public or private sale and on such terms as may seem desirable to him. Should my executor be delayed in finding a practicable sale for those portions of my estate which my trustee may designate for conversion, I authorize my executor pending such sale to rent, manage and control the same as in his judgment may seem best, without being liable for mistakes in judgment but only for gross mismanagement or negligence with the right to maintain and replenish real and personal property as he may deem necessary to keep the same both useable and saleable.

ARTICLE VII: My trustee is authorized to make loans, secured or unsecured, to the executor of my estate upon such terms as to security, rate, maturity and in other respects as it may deem advisable, and to retain the notes bonds, mortgages or other evidences of such indebtedness as trust investments without liability for loss or depreciation resulting therefrom.

ARTICLE VIII: I appoint Henry H. Rightor, Jr., executor of this my will.

In testimony whereof, I have hereunto set my hand this 6th day of November, 1939, in the presence of W.R. Orr and T.M. Short who at my request attest the same in my presence.

—S.D. WARFIELD

We, W.R. Orr and T.M. Short, do hereby certify that S.D. Warfield, the testator in the above and foregoing last will and testament subscribed the same in our presence at the time declaring to us that said instrument was his last will and testament; and we, at his request, and in his presence, and in the presence of each other, now sign our name hereto as attesting witnesses.

The Committee

Another unusual provision in S.D.'s will stated that the committee to arrange the concerts and be responsible for using the money available to them must be appointed one each by the Rabbi of Temple Beth El (at that time Rabbi Samuel Schillman), the Rector of St. John's Episcopal Church (then the Reverend Phil Leach) and the Mayor of the city of Helena (at that time Mr. Bill Stratton).

Members of the first committee were Mr. Sam Anderson, Mrs. Aubrey Solomon, and myself. Mr. Anderson, appointed by Mayor Bill Stratton, was president of KFFA Radio Station. With his knowledge of the entertainment world and of the details involved in engaging talent, he was an excellent choice. The Reverend Phil Leach of St. John's selected as his appointed member Mrs. Aubrey Solomon (Rosalind), a distinguished musician. Her dedication to the concert series is evidenced by the fact that after the death of her mother, Miss Josie, she continued to work for Civic Music Concerts. I was appointed by Rabbi Schillman and sang in the Temple Beth El Choir and also sang and sometimes directed a choir at St. John's Episcopal Church. My peers considered me to be a fine musician with a broad knowledge of the musical world.

Following S.D.'s death, Henry Haskell "Bully" Rightor, who was named executor in the will, engaged David Solomon to act as attorney for the estate. After taking care of all the details and selling the farms at auction, the funds were turned over to the Union National Bank in Little Rock as trustee. The sum was reported to be approximately $580,000. Under the terms of the will, the committee was allowed to spend up to 3% of the value of the foundation for the concerts each year.

The committee had been appointed and the funds were in place. S.D. Warfield's dream was about to come true, and Phillips County would never be the same again.

WARFIELD CONCERTS COMMITTEE MEMBERS

San Anderson—1968-74 (appointed by Mayor Stralton)

Helen Mosby—1968-69; 1970-72; 1973-75; 1976-78; 1979-81; 1982-84); 1985-87; 1988-90; 1991-93 (appointed by Rabbi Schillman)—Jewish

Rosaline Solomon—1968-70 (appointed by Phil Leach)—Episcopal

Tene Nichols—1971-73 (appointed by Phil Leach)—Episcopal

Bobbie Hornor—1974-79 (appointed by Andy Jackson)—Episcopal

Bart Lindsey—1975-77 (appointed by Mayor Thad Kelly)

Betty Faust—1978-83; 1984-86; 1987-98 (appointed by Mayor Thad Kelly)

Helen Benton—1980-85; 1986-87-88; 1989-91 (appointed by Duane Saba)—Episcopal

Cassie Brothers—1983-84-85; 1986-88; 1989-91; 1992-94; 1995-97 (appointed by Rabbi Wax)—Jewish

Betty Hendrix—1992-93; 1994-96; 1997- (appointed by Duane Saba)

Making Plans

The first meeting of the Concerts Committee took place in January 1968 at the office of Sam Anderson at the quarters of KFFA Radio Station on the fifth floor of the Solomon Building, now known as the Helena National Bank Building. The sum of $13,000 had been turned over to them to spend for concerts during that year.

The three of us sat down to talk and plan. First we would surely need someone to act as a kind of treasurer to write checks and make reports. Bessie McRee was the county treasurer and had an office in the court house. She seemed the ideal person and was glad to take over the job for $25 a month. Bessie loved all kinds of music and played the piano. She also sang in the choir at the First Presbyterian Church in Helena. These qualities enabled her to thoroughly understand and greatly enjoy the Warfield Concerts.

She had a friendly smile and a cordial greeting for all who came her way. Indeed, Bessie was loved and respected by everyone in Phillips County. She was perfect for us. However, I am sad to relate that she only lived six more years—to the age of 54. Her untimely death was a severe loss to the county as well as her many friends, but especially to me. She was my first cousin and had a very special place in my life that has never been filled.

The next decision at the meeting was to buy a piano. As Rosalind said, "We can't have concerts without a piano." She and I agreed to go to Memphis to buy one of the most impressive of all musical instruments, a nine-foot concert grand piano made by Steinway. We went to Amro Music Company, anticipating all kinds of problems, but right away we saw it in all its grandeur, our soon-to-be Steinway. It was shiny black and so beautiful. Sparkling black and white keys just waiting for some famous pianist to play. It was magnificent. A great black leather adjustable stool came with it, one that could be used by pianist big or little, tall or short. It also had a leather cover.

We traded back and forth with the final purchase price being $8,000, including delivery and a frame with rollers so that moving about was no problem.

I think the arrival of this splendid instrument can go down in history as unusual, nothing like it before or since. Upon its purchase, its new home was a little old storage room full of boxes, chairs, a couple of folding tables, various papers and all kinds of bric-a-brac. The room was attached to a so-called stage in the barn-like gymnasium of the Central High School. The movers pushed our piano in there to be kept for a few years.

The first piano concert took place in the gymnasium on Wednesday, October 1, 1969, and presented the brilliant concert pianist, Anthony di Bonaventura. I met him at the airport in Memphis and drove him to Helena, giving him on the way a glowing account of our city including its historical attractions and busy river activities. I hope he was impressed, because soon he was introduced to the stage at the Central High gym. I have often recalled that night, di Bonaventura in his white tie and tails sitting at the new piano on that bare stage before a small crowd in chairs on the floor of the gymnasium. His program had pieces from the old masters, Bach, Beethoven, and Chopin. The lovely music floated from his fingertips as they easily dashed up and down the keyboard. After concertizing in music halls in America and Europe, what could he have thought of our facilities? We will never know because he was a gentleman giving us his best. The audience responded with abundant applause and a standing ovation. Hopefully, that enthusiasm offset some of the disadvantages.

Buying a piano made a big hole in our $13,000 for 1968. However, we did manage three concerts in spite of a lack of time and money. The first one presented was the Memphis Symphony Orchestra, with guest soloist Young Uck Kim, a promising young violinist, and Maestro Vincent De Frank conducting. The event took place in the Central High gymnasium on Monday, April 22, 1968, at 8:00 P.M. This was a first for the orchestra too, the first time to play outside of Memphis. Expectations were high for both parties.

There were several big problems facing us. In 1968, mosquito control had not been very successful. The month of April brought in swarms of those stinging insects, which meant that the gymnasium would be filled with hungry mosquitoes. Well, I told the orchestra members to bring cans of insect repellant to keep under their chairs. They certainly could not play if insects were nibbling on their legs. Next, the Warfield Committee had to spend a little money to have all the broken window panes mended and chairs put in place. Most important was Mr. Ellis, the caretaker whom we called Dude, and his spray machines. He said, "Mrs. Mosby if you will get me 4 gallons of mosquito spray from the city, I will get rid of them." The City of Helena generously gave us the 4 gallons. Monday morning I found Dude in the gym going after those mosquitoes. When I went there in the afternoon I became alarmed; the atmosphere was dense with spray. I told him, "Mr. Ellis we are all going to be asphyxiated, you better stop." He then turned off the machines, and not one single mosquito appeared during the concert.

What a great time we had that night. Mr. and Mrs. Frances Thompson and Mr. and Mrs. Allen Keesee decided to give a party before the concert and invited many of S.D.'s good friends. We dressed in our best evening clothes just as he would have wanted us to do had he been with us. He loved to dress formally and made a great occasion of most social activities to which he added his warm personality and charm.

The concert drew a large crowd of hand-clapping people. As Luciano Pavarotti once said, "The applause is my oxygen." So it seemed with the symphony. The applause pleased them for they did a superb performance, particularly in the Saint-Seans concerto when Young Uck Kim came forth with his delicate dreamy violin tones.

The night ended with a reception at the Mosby home in honor of the orchestra. The Warfield committee felt that their first concert was a success.

The other two concerts that year were the United States Marine Band on November 13th and the Roger Wagner Chorale on November 19th. Both of these concerts were held in the gym.

Having performed numerous times at the White House, the Marine Band is considered by many to be the best concert band of all the military forces. They did both an afternoon and evening performance, boosting our patriotism to a higher level and inspiring the Central High School boys to consider a career in the marines.

The Roger Wagner chorale was a formal well-dressed group of men and women who sang to perfection the classical music which S.D. loved. As they performed, they seemed to remember these words from his will: "A perpetual charitable trust to promote the education and aesthetic enjoyment of the community in which this estate has been accumulated."

Through the years, we have always had tickets, even though the concerts are free. We first placed the tickets at the banks, the library, and the Chamber of Commerce. Anyone could stop by and get a ticket as long as tickets lasted. Also, one could send in a self-addressed stamped envelope and receive up to four tickets by mail.

The two old sayings, "To learn the hard way," and "Experience is the best teacher," apply to our tickets.

We tried to be as much like the theater as possible. The tickets were printed with a blank spot for the rows and a blank spot for the seat numbers. I then filled in by hand the numbers so that each chair had a ticket. The idea was that one could choose a seat when asking for a ticket. It is easy to imagine that ushers were somewhat confused. Thinking back, I wonder how they managed.

When the gym was no longer used, we gave up our difficult seating arrangement. No more numbers and rows. The tickets for each concert were similar, but the color of the tickets changed for each concert. It did not take long to use all available colors. I never did decide on my favorite ticket color, maybe pale blue or lemon yellow. I did (learning from experience) realize that black print on red and dark green is hard to read and that shocking pink is just too shocking. Lavender is nice for a piano trio or bright royal blue for a large group.

Finally, what seemed to be the right way arrived. Now, there is one ticket for the entire season. The name and the date of each concert is printed on the same ticket. It is larger than the old ones and requires only one mailing.

People have frequently asked, "Why do you have tickets?" There are several reasons, one being that the size of the crowd can be judged by the number of tickets given out. I am glad to say that a nice number of out-of-town people attend the concerts. These people feel more secure with a ticket. They also immensely appreciate the opportunity given them. Tickets make a concert a little more special than just saying "come one come all." It is best to have tickets. Also concert goers must, in the near future, "be sure to get ... concert tickets at the Chamber of Commerce which handles all of them now."

Five years later, on April 22, 1973, the Memphis Symphony Orchestra came back to Helena to play for a concert in our new Lily Peter Auditorium. The following are the welcoming remarks I made before the concert:

WELCOME

I would like to welcome everyone tonight to another Warfield Concert and a very particular welcome to our out-of-town visitors. We have quite a large group from Memphis and many others from neighboring towns in Arkansas and Mississippi. We appreciate your coming and hope you will enjoy the concert.

We are very fortunate to have for our program tonight the ENTIRE Memphis Symphony Orchestra conducted by Maestro Vicent de Frank with guest artists Miss Berverly Wolfe and Mr. John Stuart.

There is a little something very special about tonight's concert. Five years ago this very month on a Monday night the Memphis Symphony Orchestra came to Helena to perform for the first Warfield Concert ever given. They played in a barn-like gymnasium on an extremely crowded stage. There were broken window panes and the stage curtain was torn. But the worst of it all was the mosquitoes—everywhere. And after the concert was over our Warfield Committee made a promise—that one of these days we would invite them back to play in a nice auditorium—not having any idea when that would be.

Tonight we are keeping our promise. Members of the Symphony we thank you for coming back and we are going to enjoy your beautiful music.

During the next two years, the Warfield Committee

tried their best to have a variety of selections to please everyone (including those very hard-to-please people) with at least one concert that they would thoroughly enjoy even though the idea necessitated moving a little away from the original intent of the will. The choice ranged from Ruth Page's International Ballet, considered one of the best, to Jack Greene, Jeanie Sealy, and the Jolly Giants of Country. Still more contrast was offered in a concert by the famous trumpeter Harry James and his band.

The three of us on the Warfield Committee were of the generation that could remember Harry James when he was in his prime during the mid-forties taking his band tunes for dances and shows everywhere. He made his name as a star-playing trumpeter with Benny Goodman's Orchestra. Then, he branched out with a band of his own. Adding to his popularity was his wife, the glamorous film star, Betty Grable, whose legs were insured for one million dollars with Lloyd's of London. She and Harry were reported to be very much in love and devoted to each other.

He had a good friend here, Helenian Sonny Payne, who gave the event extra publicity through his work at the local KFFA Radio Station. Sonny entertained with a fine party after the concert in honor of Harry James and his band.

There were many out-of-town visitors (mainly from Memphis) who had fond memories of him, but he had changed with the years. Following the popular trend for more noise, there were microphones on every instrument. The result was LOUD and LOUDER. Certainly, the gymnasium acoustics did nothing but accentuate the condition.

At intermission, I went behind the stage and pleaded with him to tone it down, but he refused, saying, "It stays like it is or we do not play." His abrupt reply was a little startling, but he had enjoyed a career of enormous success, and I supposed he had reached an age when he did not care to be bothered with suggestions.

The large crowd apparently enjoyed the performance in spite of the deafening sound. They smiled and applauded, and I think the evening could be called successful.

We heard that West Point Military Academy would sing free of charge. "Wonderful!" was the remark. "We'll add them to our 1970 spring schedule. They would be delighted to come we were told. They did not object to singing in the gym. How easy this was going to be. We agreed on the date, March 7th, 8 P.M. All was well.

We soon learned that all was not well. In order to come to Helena, the trip must be made by plane and the Warfield Committee would be responsible for the traveling cost. It amounted to more than $4,000. This shocking price caused a real snag in our plans, but finally we bravely agreed to assume the expense.

There were no regrets. Those young male voices produced a rich beautiful sound, ending the concert

with an unusual arrangement of "The Battle Hymn of
the Republic" by Julia Ward Howe, a piece that can
touch hearts as well as bring a few tears to some eyes.
For even those with their emotions under control, it
was thrilling to hear. Some of the lines used solo voices but all five verses were sung, and the chorus
brought out a rousing march tempo with the words
"Glory, glory hallelujah! His truth is marching on."

Almost nine months in advance, a contract was
negotiated and completed by Columbia Artists
Management, Inc. between Warfield Concerts and The
National Symphony Orchestra Conducted by Arthur
Fiedler, with Jeffrey Siegel, guest pianist, for a concert
in Helena on Sunday night, March 28, 1971, at eight
o'clock. The fee of $6,000 to be paid the night of the
concert was satisfactory. With inflated prices as we
now have in the nineties it is hard to believe that such
a figure could be achieved, but $6,000 was what we
paid for one of the most exciting concerts in all my
many years on the Warfield Committee. The following
description of Arthur Fiedler, The National Symphony
Orchestra, and Jeffrey Siegel is taken from the program notes for the March 28, 1971 concert.

With appreciation we said, "Goodbye" to the
Central High Gym and Dude Ellis who had been valuable help with our performances there. Holding my
breath for fear of a slip, I watched local movers take
the nine-foot Steinway from its packed-in quarters,
place it on a truck with ropes, and very slowly and

carefully put down in the new gymnasium at Phillips County Community College. I breathed a sigh of relief as my thoughts gave a silent prayer of thanksgiving that the move had been completed without mishap.

There it was in the recently completed building, with freshly painted walls, new fairly comfortable bleachers, and a smoothly sanded and varnished floor glistening with cleanliness just awaiting the arrival of Mr. Music and his orchestra.

At about 2 P.M., two buses came to a stop at the Holiday Inn where the big outside electric sign read WELCOME NATIONAL SYMPHONY ORCHESTRA AND ARTHUR FIELDER. Musicians and instruments filled the lobby. "Where is the Maestro?" I wanted to know. "He's coming behind us," said the bus driver, "with Siegel and the concert master in a private car." Very soon the door opened as all three walked in.

Checking in for a private suite, Mr. Fiedler was given a little note that I had left in his box, "I would like to invite you and a few members of the Orchestra to a small reception at my home after the concert."

He called immediately, and I quickly realized from his conversation that Arthur Fiedler liked parties. "How many can I bring with me?" he asked. Of course, I could not accommodate the entire ninety piece symphony, but I told him that twelve to fifteen would be very nice to have (I think about twenty players came).

Arthur Fiedler always knew how to charm an audience. His carefully selected program was enjoyed by everyone. Somewhat surprising to the classical music lovers in the audience was the group of three Beatle tunes. I particularly remember how my dear friend, Miss Lily Peter, whom I loved, was a little more than surprised to find Beatle music on the program. Miss Lily used to say that Jazz music made her physically ill. She would listen to lighter composers such as the Straus family or forms of South American dances, but she did not ever forgive Arthur Fiedler for those Beatle tunes.

According to the program notes, "various commentators have been trying to settle the question, 'What remains of value from the popular music of the past ten years?'" Agreement is unanimous that new and valuable contributions were made by the Beatles. Joining in this consensus is Mr. Fiedler. He was one of the first classically-oriented musicians to appreciate the fresh, invigorating productions of the Beatles. Quickly introducing their music at the Boston Pops, he was rewarded by continuing demands for a repetition.

These three tunes were played one after the other without any break in the music. As each one was heard, a sign on a long pole was held up in the middle of the musicians with the title of the tune on it. The performance was unique and appealed to the audience.

My husband, Winston, and I rushed home after the concert to be there ahead of the guests. On the way I said, "Winston, this is to be a very proper party. For drinks we will have punch and coffee. I'm sure Arthur Fiedler would not want it otherwise. How wrong that statement was. When the front door opened and our celebrity guest was asked, "Maestro, what would you like, some punch or coffee?" "I'll have bourbon on the rocks, please," was the reply. He walked through the crowd speaking graciously and took a seat in my little breakfast room with his bourbon which I had hurriedly produced.

There he sat with Jeffrey Siegel for two hours in friendly conversation, touching on politics, our town, and some of his traveling experiences. Since Winston had the honor of being their chauffeur to go back to the motel, he began to worry about the time and was glad when he heard Jeffrey say, "Maestro, we are playing in Jackson (Tennessee) tomorrow. I think it is time for us to go." Reluctantly, we said goodby to our new friend, but what a wonderful night we had. Spring was in the air, and the stars twinkled brightly as if they too had enjoyed the music. In my home had been one of the greatest musicians of the century.

Arthur Fiedler died in 1979. He conducted the Boston Pops almost to his last days. To those who knew him, he left an indelible memory. To younger generations who will read about him, I hope they will be able to conceive to some degree his unique qualities and influence on the musical world.

The Fine Arts Center, Part I

October 1968. The time had come. No longer could the idea of a fine arts center be just a dream. The dream, somehow, had to become true.

I can remember my own grandiose visions of another opera house, or music hall. My mind's eye saw an impressive brick structure. Inside there would be gold-trimmed red plush seats filling the main floor, a balcony, and special boxes at each side. Crystal chandeliers would add another touch of elegance. Soft red carpeting in the aisles would brighten the path of the well-dressed spectators as they were seated. The stage would be closed off with a handsome velvet curtain. The acoustics would be perfect, making the most soft-spoken dialogue audible. Of course, nothing of such magnificence could ever become a reality. My dream faded, and in its place, I saw the Central High School gymnasium. That was the reality.

Being one of the three members of the Warfield Concerts Committee, I was often asked, "What can we do about an auditorium or a theater or, even better, a fine arts center?"

Paul Oliver of the Phillips County Chamber of Commerce had told me that two conventions were turned down because we had no meeting hall. There was no comfortable place for chamber banquets or Junior Auxiliary balls or sales meetings. One Sunday after church, Mr. Tully Hornor, Sr., owner of West-Hornor Motor Co. and one of Helena's respected "older citizens" said, "We have just got to have a community center. You try to do something about it." There were many more remarks of this nature going around. Some were quite forceful. Others were simply bits of conversation, but enough had been said to give me the needed "push."

Consequently, I soon awakened one morning and told myself "Get busy!" By 10:00 A.M. I was dressed and on my way to the office of Dr. John Easley, President of Phillips County Community College. After exchanging "Good Mornings" and a few brief words and not wanting to impose on the valuable time of our college president, I proceeded, "Please do not think I have become insane (his pleasant expression encouraged me to continue). If I can call together a representative group of Phillips County citizens for the purpose of discussing the building of a fine arts center, may we meet here at the college?" "Of course," he quickly replied, "and I will meet with them." It was my turn to have a pleasant expression and give my nervous

system a rest. I happily concluded, "Thank you a thousand times. You will hear from me soon."

About twenty-five people attended the first meeting. "A wonderful idea," they all agreed, but next time
when we met for more discussions the number was
smaller. Finally, there were only ten left who were
determined to accomplish our ambitious task. They
were Mr. Carlos Smith, Administrator of the Helena
Hospital; Mrs. Tom Choate, whose husband owned the
Ford Motor Co.; Mrs. David Solomon, wife of attor-
ney David Solomon; Mrs. Aubrey (Rosalind)
Solomon, choir director of Temple Beth El; the Rev.
C.W. Cartwright, pastor of the First Presbyterian
Church; Mr. William H. Brandon, president of the
First National Bank of Phillips County; Mr. John
King, a farmer; Dr. John Easley, President of PCCC;
Mr. Thad Kelly, Mayor of Helena; and myself, repre-
senting the Warfield Concerts Committee. We asked
Carlos Smith to act as Chairman, and we called our-
selves the Steering Committee for the Phillips County
Community Center. All agreed that it was probably the
largest undertaking our county had ever attempted.

Several times we consulted the Board of Trustees
of the Phillips County Community College who
agreed to make available the land for our building. Dr.
John Easley informed the committee that there would
be a strong possibility of receiving a federal grant to be
applied toward the construction costs of the building if
we could raise the initial $300,000 locally. In addition,

the College Board would seek to secure a low rate loan to be paid off over a forty-year period to make up the balance needed for the million-dollar structure.

With this in mind, we were confronted with the problem of raising the $300,000. Taxation and bond issues were discussed. The problem was that with a bond issue it would have to be done by the City of Helena who would then have to own the building, and the City of Helena did not have any land to build it on or any way to keep it up after it was built. Neither would the City of Helena be eligible for a federal grant.

We then decided to get advice from other citizens throughout the county. One hundred people were personally interviewed by members of the Steering Committee concerning their opinion about our project. They were asked such questions as "Do you think we need a community center?" "Do you think the money should be raised by taxation or contributions?" "Are you willing to work for such an undertaking?" Responses to these questions were reviewed and carefully analyzed, and the results were overwhelmingly in favor of a fund-raising campaign.

In the meantime, Aubrey Scott, one of the architects of the firm of Stuck and Associates in Jonesboro, Arkansas, was selected by the Steering Committee and the College Board to do the architectural drawings for the center. He promised to start work immediately. More time-consuming meetings, discussions, and investigations took place. The time required for these matters was gladly and cheerfully given by those who participated. In my opinion, Part I had been accomplished, and the fund-raising must begin.

The Fine Arts Center, Part II

The Steering Committee sat around the large, handsome mahogany table in the Board Room of Phillips County Community College. We looked at each other and decided, "We cannot go out of here and start asking for donations without first making our own pledges." There was no objection to that procedure. Then, one by one, we spoke out in front of the others and declared our pledge. The total sum amounted, as I remember, to $9,350. A start had been made.

It was decided to establish a fund-raising committee chosen from among the 100 local citizens interviewed in the public survey. Fourteen people accepted a position on the Committee to raise funds, but none of them would be the Chairman, who certainly needed to have a strong, capable personality and the time and determination to lead the way. The best person we could think of to do that job was Miss Lily Peter. They looked at me. "Do you think your friend Miss Lily could be persuaded to do this?"

Miss Lily, Poet Laureate of Arkansas, writer, musician, successful farmer and excellent business woman, had just returned from a whirlwind round of national appearances due to the prominence she had received from bringing the Philadelphia Orchestra conducted by world-famous Eugene Ormandy to Little Rock, Arkansas, for two consecutive evening concerts. She had paid out of her own pocket $45,000 for this unique history-making event. Admission to the concerts was $5 per ticket. The money from the sale of tickets was given to the universities in the state. It is easy to imagine the explosion that took place. Photographers and reporters came from "far and wide." She was photographed in every conceivable way—from riding a tractor in party clothes to chopping cotton or reading her poetry. Everyone wanted her to be on "their program." She had been escorted from one place to another, including the cities of Dallas and Fort Worth, Texas, where she was extremely well received.

The excitement of these occasions would surely have wearied her beyond assuming a responsibility of the magnitude required to lead a fund-raising drive for a fine arts center. In spite of the circumstances, we decided to call on this wonderful lady and ask.

Carlos Smith, Bill Cartwright, and I were the trio sent to her home in the country below Marvell, Arkansas, to approach the subject. On the way, we feared, "Suppose she said no?" But we hoped and asked. At least in our favor was a beautiful day in May

1969. Arriving exactly at the appointed hour, there she was on the porch of her tiny white house, a petite figure as fresh as the flowers in her yard, waiting to give us her usual gracious welcome and looking far younger than her 78 years.

So loyal was Miss Lily to the cotton industry that she insisted on wearing cotton clothing as much as possible. On that particular day, she wore a pink cotton dress with a lace collar. The first impression a stranger might have of her would be a feeling of quaintness, like a breath of lavender and old lace, but not for long. Her face reflected a strong character and a depth of intelligence. She knew everything and seemed to remember everything she had ever learned. There were those flashing dark brown eyes with their heavy eyebrows and a mouth that could be firm yet always speaking tactfully with ladylike gentleness in a voice that had almost a musical quality. During the years of our friendship, not once did I ever see her angry or use inappropriate words. Whatever the situation, she kept herself well controlled.

"How lovely to see you," she greeted us. "Let's sit on the porch and enjoy the warm air." Carlos and Bill began a polite casual conversation, but my "stick-to-the-point" nature interrupted.

"Miss Lily, we have completed plans to build a fine arts center. We desperately need a chairman to take charge of the fund-raising. Would you be that person?"

Without the slightest hesitation, she answered, "I

would be honored and happy to do it." I wanted to stand up and cheer. Instead, I settled for a big hug and profuse "thank you's." Carlos and Bill added more "thank you's." We were elated and relieved. Right then and there we decided the first meeting would be the next week at the hospitality room of the Arkansas Power and Light building.

Mrs. Fred Faust, Sr., who retired after her many years of service at the First National Bank, agreed to be Secretary and Treasurer. This was an important position for which she was well qualified to take care of the records and the collections as they were brought in. We kept her busy. She always smiled a very genuine smile that reflected a spirit of friendliness and enthusiasm. Mrs. Faust (or just Alma to her family and close friends) lived to be well into her nineties. Throughout her life, she remained a loyal citizen and a devoted member of the West Helena Baptist Church.

Mr. J.P. "Doc" Baker, of the law firm Baker and Pittman, let us use his copy machine and sometimes his secretary for important letters. We consumed pounds and pounds of his paper and hours of his time. Doc was an important member of the fund-raising committee. Particularly, he was successful in obtaining donations from former Helenians who had moved away. Their pledges amounted to a considerable sum.

Miss Lily, at her first meeting, enlisted a large number of willing workers to assist the Fund-Raising Committee. She also announced that several big donations would be forthcoming if we had a successful drive by raising the initial $300,000. She called those "challenge-gifts."

The drive was successful. In March of 1971, the formal ground-breaking ceremony for the $1,200,000 Fine Arts Center at Phillips Community College took place. In one part of it was the fulfillment of our dream—a beautiful auditorium which we named The Lily Peter Auditorium.

How interesting it was to watch our building grow, rising from the ground brick by brick in front of the green hillside and wooded background that blossomed in springtime with dogwood and redbud amid stately oak trees, spreading their graceful branches for summer shade followed by brilliant color in the fall. Those molded red blocks were laid with amazing speed, if good weather prevailed. We also had our wet spells of drizzle and drenching rain familiar to inhabitants of river towns. That discouraging moisture frequently brought the remarks, "It will never be finished," and "Ten years from now, they will still be at it." No matter what part the weather played or what the public thought, said, or did, the builders kept their promise. By the fall of 1972, there stood our beautiful Phillips County Community College Fine Arts Center, ready to be used and enjoyed.

A few steps led to the entrance, a row of sturdy glass doors opening into a spacious lobby. On the right side of the lobby was an enormous reception hall which has been used almost constantly for activities varying from student gatherings to formal wedding receptions. The most recent occasion was a one hundredth birthday party honoring Mr. Alvin Solomon, Helena's oldest citizen. About 400 friends gathered there to wish him well as he stood on a platform and used a microphone to greet all of them. He treated himself to a new car for a final birthday present. Alvin neither looks nor acts his age and is a loyal friend.

Across the lobby facing the front door was the Red Room, a small meeting room so named because the walls were covered with rich red carpeting. The room's acoustics were excellent. Track lights made it a perfect place for painting exhibitions or other displays. On each side of the red room were more heavy glass doors that opened the way to a *porte cochere.*

The crown jewel of the center was the Lily Peter Auditorium. On the wall between its two entrances were numerous small brass name plates, representing those who had contributed to the fund-raising drive, and a head sculpture of Miss Lily Peter in brass bas-relief. More than once she told me, "It does not look like me. I intend to have a new one made," but she passed one hundred years without ever doing so.

Inside, on the main floor and balcony, there were 1,200 seats. On the top of the orchestra pit that bordered the broad adequate stage was a larger brass plate with a most appropriate inscription—IN MEMORY OF SAMUEL DRAKE WARFIELD.

The Dedication

Phillips County Community College and Warfield Foundation Concerts joined forces in a celebration and dedication of the Fine Arts Center and the Lily Peter Auditorium on Sunday night, December 3, 1972, at 8:00 P.M.

A glorious time of year for using Christmas decor, the Auditorium was resplendent in green and red; wreaths of holly and cedar had been placed along the walls; across the front of the Samuel Drake Warfield stage were garlands of pine draped and accented with generous double-size red velvet bows. The joyous spirit of the occasion was clearly evident.

In the center of the stage was Miss Lily Peter in her elegant white lace gown with a large showy orchid on her shoulder. She was at her best, sparkling with enthusiasm and full of conversation over the many compliments coming her way. The others in line with her were the Rev. W. Bill Cartwright, Mrs. Fred Faust, Mrs. Helen Mosby, United States Senator John L. McClellan from Arkansas and guest, and Mr. E. Clay Bumpers of Wabash, Arkansas, who was a member of the college board.

Opening the program, Mrs. Faust and I spoke very briefly, making only a few introductory Welcomes and Thank-Yous in view of the fact that much more would be said and heard in the course of the evening.

After Mr. Cartwright's invocation, Miss Lily came to the microphone to speak before the audience of about eight hundred people who were eagerly waiting to hear her.

Miss Lily had an unlimited vocabulary (I used to think she knew every word in the dictionary) and the intellect to express herself with excellent phraseology. Her words flowed freely this historic occasion. Her talk was a little longer than we had anticipated, but everyone was in a happy mood, so that time was not a problem.

However, under cover of rousing applause and the presentation of two dozen red roses, one of the members of the orchestra who had grown restless waiting to play ventured to say very quietly, "It is nine o'clock, but after all this is her auditorium and she can do anything she likes." She made one more bow before we left the stage to the Arkansas Symphony Orchestra. Conductor Dr. Francis McBeth, walked to the podium, bowed to the approbation of the crowd, turned back, giving the downbeat for his musicians, and the performance began.

The Warfield Committee decided to present the Arkansas Symphony in concert for this special night because Miss Lily frequently had given generous financial support to the orchestra, particularly during the periods of organization and development. She regularly came to their rescue when funds were needed.

Since Miss Lily had not only a love for the violin but had studied violin at the noted Julliard School of Music and could play quite well herself, the talented violinist Guy Lumia was engaged to be the guest artist with the orchestra. He completely charmed Miss Lily by playing one of her favorite Concertos for the violin by Mendelssohn. In later years she gave her highly rated violin to the Arkansas Symphony.

After the concert, Winston and I entertained with a reception at our house on Stonebrook Road inviting as many out-of-town guests as possible. The nicest one of them all spent the night with us and her name was Miss Lily Peter.

A free Warfield Concert and a new music hall being dedicated and named after a lady who had gained national recognition was enough to have newspaper representatives arriving in town from a number of big publishing companies.

Among them was Roy Reed of the *New York Times*. His article brought forth a full page story with photographs in the *New York Times* dated Wednesday, December 6, 1972. The headlines read, HELENA, ARK. AN EMBRYONIC CENTER OF MUSIC.

His story began with the opening paragraph:

Helena, Ark., Dec. 5—A hundred years from now, when history records how this Mississippi River town of 21,422 (these 21,422 residents live in adjoining municipalities, Helena and West Helena, but speak of them as one place) became a famous musical center during the last quarter of the 20th century there is a risk that the story will bedismissed as Jack and the Beanstalk legend .... The fruits of the beanstalk are already visible. Sunday night the town dedicated a new one million dollar auditorium that was a direct outgrowth of the Warfield legacy. Van Cliburn is coming to play a free concert in February.

The Arkansas Symphony Orchestra played Beethoven, Mendelssohn, Shostakovich, and John Frederick Peter, the last a Moravian ancestor of the Arkansas woman for whom the auditorium was named. After the concert Mr. Warfield's friends had a party and talked about him.

Having to spend so much money on music has stretched the cultural perimeters of placid Helena (pronounced HEL-nah). The town, in spite of its slogan, "Arkansas' only seaport," has grown very little in recent years.

Since it was founded in 1820, it has not concerned itself with much beyond gracious living and the price of cotton.

There was, of course, that interruption in 1861 when Federal troops were all over town keeping an eye on the river traffic, and Confederate troops were in the countryside trying sporadically and unsuccessfully to get in, but that is almost forgotten now.

Roy Reed can think the Battle of Helena has been forgotten even though it is mentioned in some Civil War history books. The fact is that the conflict left scars and those scars are now interesting tourist attractions.

I told my good friend, Mrs. Virginia Straub, who is a columnist with our local paper, the *Daily World*, about the *New York Times* story. This is what she had to say:

> Helena was indeed a sleepy little town described by Roy Reed in the New York Times article in 1972 and depending on the time of year the outsider sees it, may still appear so. But something happened soon after the Warfield Concert Series began. Perhaps it was the strangers who came here and kept telling us we "had something here" and gradually as more and more tourists came to see what is was the town began developing those things. Enter tourism.

Both the batteries where the Battle of Helena was fought on July 3, 1863, and the cemetery where soldiers of both the Confederacy and the Union are buried attract many visitors.

Among the graves on the top of Confederate Hill is a large elaborate monument in honor of General Patrick Cleburne and a tall obelisk dedicated to the memory of General Thomas C. Hindman, which stands at the turn of Cemetery Drive. They were two of the seven generals from Phillips County who fought in the War Between the States. The other five were Generals Lucius E. Pol, James C. Tappan, Daniel C. Govan, Charles W. Adams, and Archibald S. Dobbins.

For years after the Civil War, there was an organization here called the Seven Generals Chapter of the United Daughters of the Confederacy. The backbone of this group was Mrs. Fannie Mae Hornor, a true lady and patriotic Southerner. After her death in the sixties, it no longer existed.

The local historical society began sponsoring tours of historical places and homes in the late 1970s, a movement which served to awaken the community to the potential of developing interest in its past.

In 1986, Warfield Concerts added a Spring Music Festival to their regular season, and in October of that year, the first King Biscuit Blues Festival took place. Both of these events have brought many visitors to the Helenas. Helena is no longer Roy Reed's "sleepy little town."

In the first quarter of this century, Helena, Arkansas, flourished. Because of the abundance of extremely fine hardwood, several sawmills and lumber companies including Chicago Mill and Lumber Company, were established here. As the timber was cut away, the rich land was developed into prosperous cotton farms. River boats brought in more business, an opera house was built, Habib's fine restaurant shipped fruit cake all over the nation, a race track and stables existed in North Helena, and the price of cotton was nearing one dollar a pound.

Sadly, the stock market crash in 1929 and the Great Depression of the early nineteen thirties brought an end to much of our glory days. But one quality we have never lost: the friendliness of the people has remained passing from one generation to another. The people of Phillips County have the ability to courteously welcome strangers with genuine friendliness that is appealing. We make visitors feel good without using "rose-colored glasses" to do it. They like to come here, and we like them, too.

Turnip Greens and Cornbread

February 5, 1973: turnip greens and corn bread went to the concert. Yes, they really did and sat down on the front row of the Lily Peter Auditorium with the largest crowd ever assembled for a Warfield performance. That includes up to the present date of this writing. How dearly S.D. would have loved this auspicious occasion. Surely his spirit was right there enjoying every aspect of it.

For additional accommodations, seventy-five chairs had been put on the stage (so placed with the knowledge and permission of the artist). The orchestra pit was filled with seats and there was an extra chair in the aisle at the end of every row. People were even sitting on the few steps at each side of the stage. It was a massive crowd, including Governor and Mrs. Bumpers and numerous other prominent executives in Arkansas. Word had spread far and wide. It seemed as if everyone in the world wanted a free ticket.

Mrs. Cappi Lindsey had charge of the tickets where

they could be obtained at the Chamber of Commerce. She reported, "The telephone was ringing constantly. When I finally had to say there were no more tickets ugly words came back at me. People were furious!" We did the best we could and were able to seat all ticket holders but it was a close call.

The clock pointed to 8:00 P.M., the usual starting time for every concert. Suddenly the situation was critical. The artist for the evening was the superstar of classical pianists at that date, the great world-renowned Van Cliburn, and he had not yet arrived in town.

In the wings of the stage stood the Warfield Committee, Sam Anderson, Tene Nichols (Mrs. Hal Nichols appointed when Rosalind resigned because of ill health), and me wringing our hands in despair and not knowing what to do. We knew that Van Cliburn had been in Memphis that day at the Rivermont. We also had been told that he liked to arrive in town just before concert time.

I had been uneasy all day, feeling that something like this could happen. In the afternoon, I called the Rivermont at about 5:00 P.M. Mr. Cliburn was still there, but his three Memphis friends who had insisted on driving him to Helena assured me not to worry: "We have plenty of time. We will be there." My reply to those supposedly comforting words, "If you have car trouble, what then?" More encouraging talk, "We are coming in two cars for that very reason."

There we were without Van Cliburn. My fears rose and my heart sank. How could I face that multitude and tell them "No Cliburn, No concert"? I thought to myself, "This calamity is all my fault. The concert was my idea and I handled the entire negotiations. I am the cause of all our trouble. I must face it."

Sam decided he could hold the audience for a few more minutes by introducing the governor of Arkansas. So out he bravely went to the front stage, hiding his anxiety with the appearance of a confident master of ceremonies, to ask Governor and Mrs. Dale Bumpers to stand for recognition. Seconds were ticking away when suddenly the stage door opened and there stood our delinquent Van Cliburn. I looked at him in not a very pleasant way and sternly said, "You're late!"

He heard the end of Sam's introduction and bracing himself, replied, "Should not have kept the governor waiting." As Sam joined us Van asked him to go back and adjust the piano stool. "You'll have to do that yourself," was Sam's reaction. The committee returned to our front row seats, Van Cliburn marched out, adjusted the stool, sat down and played "The Star Spangled Banner," which he regularly did as an opener for all his concerts.

The next hour and thirty minutes took us to a dream world of beautiful music as he played pieces by Brahms, Beethoven, and Chopin, concluding the program in a lighter vein with the familiar Clair de Lune, a work of the French composer Claude Debussy. His hands moved up and down the keyboard. From the first note on through the recital, the listeners were enchanted. That tall handsome man seated gracefully at the Steinway met our highest expectations. He proved himself the legend he had become, a great musician and one that knew instantly how to capture an audience.

During the intermission, I took a quick look inside my large evening bag to see about my nice tender turnip greens which had been cooked in the afternoon and stored in a neat little glass jar. Then I called to my friend Hazel King (Mrs. Clancy King), "How is the corn bread doing?"

She also took a quick little peek in her bag and said "Fine, still looks fresh." That was a relief because the turnip greens and corn bread had to go to a reception.

The city of Helena wanted the famous pianist who had dazzled Russia to remember us. After the recital, the Chamber of Commerce gave a big reception at the Helena Country Club in his honor. To be certain he would accept such a party, I had called his New York Manager, Sol Hurak, and was told that he would be very happy to attend if, immediately after the performance, he could have a substantial meal. I asked for his preference in food. What he would most enjoy would be some turnip greens and corn bread, and that is what he had—plus a big juicy steak.

He was served in the pro-shop of the Country Club.

The door was tightly shut, and I stood on guard with both arms stretched out across it to keep back the frantic crowd, each individual trying to be the first to offer greetings.

Very soon, he opened the door coming out with a big smile, relaxed and ready to accept the praise and attention awaiting him. He hugged the elderly ladies who adored him and shook hands with the men, receiving everyone with the graciousness and charm of a well-born gentleman who would be remembered for years to come.

This whole event could not have taken place without the financial assistance of our generous Miss Lily Peter. She had heard me mention several times how thrilling it would be to present Van Cliburn for a Warfield Concert, but the price was $8,500, an amount impossible for us to pay.

One night a few weeks after our conversation the telephone rang and there was Miss Lily's voice: "My dear, I've been thinking about Van Cliburn. I want you to go ahead and engage him for a performance. I will pay half of the fee."

What good news! I was so elated and almost speechless but did say, "Oh! Miss Lily, how wonderful! Thank you a thousand times. This will be great."

"Well," she continued, "I want the auditorium to get off to a good start and this is the very way to do it." Without Miss Lily's help, Van Cliburn's visit would not have happened.

The reception did not last long. Of course it was after ten o'clock when it started. The crowd soon began to thin, and by eleven forty-five, Miss Lily, Van Cliburn, and I were the only remaining guests. The two of them were quickly forming a lasting friendship. They decided to have a little candle light supper consisting mainly of coffee and a sweet with a lot of conversation. Not being a coffee drinker, I found a comfortable chair and waited because Miss Lily was my overnight visitor. I think Van Cliburn was fascinated with Miss Lily. Her brilliant mind could surely impress the most highly educated. Van Cliburn evidently thought so too because the next two years at Christmas time he sent her large arrangements of beautiful fresh red roses.

I have been interested in keeping up with his career. He finally had to have a break from the exhausting schedule and took a much needed rest for quite a long time.

His beloved Mother, Rildia Bee O'Bryan Cliburn, who guided him from his childhood, died a few years ago. She was well into her nineties. As a final tribute a large symphony orchestra played at her funeral.

Note to the reader: Van Cliburn's story is related exactly as it really happened. The quotations are true and accurate—no exaggerations, no fabrications.

High Water

We had another crisis in the very next event that followed the Van Cliburn concert. As usual, something difficult developed. This time, we were powerless over the situation. What could be done about a flood inside Lily Peter Auditorium during a performance? The answer was obviously, "Nothing."

For two consecutive nights, March 9th and 10th, 1973, the University Theater Workshop at Fayetteville, Arkansas, brought to Helena an opera, *The Bartered Bride* by Bedrich Smetana (1824-1884). Known for his national Bohemian music, he was a composer loved and admired by his fellow countrymen. Paul Stefan has said, "Smetana may be considered the hero of Czech music, not only its great founder, but its guardian spirit and gifted architect."

The Bartered Bride was fully staged with a forty-seven-piece opera orchestra. Most of the principals were double cast as is customary with student productions when the opera is being done two evenings in a row. There was one exception. Dr. Maxwell Worthley, the overall director, sang the leading male role of Hans both nights. He had a pleasing, well-trained tenor voice. Although the libretto was originally written in the Czechoslovakian language, the student cast sang it in English.

The setting for *The Bartered Bride* was a village in Bohemia in the middle of the nineteenth century. Spring was in the air, and matchmakers were busy. The humorous plot and folk flavor of the music had an appeal to our local audience. It was the first time many of them had ever had an opera experience. Their response clearly expressed approval.

All went well opening night except for a little rain, not enough to diminish the size of the crowd, who laughed and clapped all evening. We, the Warfield Committee, were beaming with pride over the success of our first opera presentation. We looked forward to the following night, feeling stimulated for another grand production and sizable attendance.

My anticipation took a downward turn the next morning when I looked out the window to see heavy clouds and sheets of rain.

How could this be happening? Wet, wetter, and wettest. All three degrees of that adjective were not enough to describe the downpour. "Perhaps it will blow over," I tried to be optimistic, "but the month of March is noted for winds and thunderstorms."

Hourly, I checked the forecast only to hear, "Heavy showers and a possibility of flash floods." We did not have any flash floods, although the rain continued through the day, making a heavy burden on the city's drainage system. My feeling of apprehension continued.

By late afternoon, there was just a little drizzle. I felt hopeful now that it would stop before opening time and let those people who "dare not venture out in bad weather" come to the opera.

I dressed hurriedly; Winston could take his time over supper. I had to eat quickly and get to the auditorium to see what might have happened. As a child, I was told not to eat my food so fast. My parents warned me, "You will swallow your supper whole." However that is about what I did, and then I left.

Well, we were going to have an audience. Approaching the Fine Arts Center, I could see cars lined up and passengers getting out. Raincoats and umbrellas were in abundance. Some had been there the night before and had come back again, bringing friends with them. The word must have been passed around that we had a good opera. The dampness did not seem to matter. The lobby was crowded, and I decided to go ahead and take my usual seat on the front row next to Tene and Hal Nichols. My dear husband Winston did not care for classical music and definitely did not like opera. Because of me, he would show at the concert—albeit for only a few minutes. He would wait until almost curtain time. Then, well-shaved, graying hair brushed neatly back, dressed in his Sunday best, white shirt, pretty tie and dark suit,

Winston's pattern was to walk slowly all the way down the aisle, speaking to friends along the way, to where I was seated. Instead of joining me, he took a left turn, walked across the front row and up the opposite aisle, out the door, and back home he went. The inimitable Winston Mosby had been to the concert.

It was all right with me if that was what he wanted to do. I was always busy keeping up with what was going on, sometimes a trip backstage or finding a seat for someone or reporting that people were either too hot or too cold. Continual interruptions there were.

As we waited, I turned to Tene and whispered, "You know that the orchestra pit has several damp spots on the floor. Maybe it had a good scrubbing today." She decided to stand up and see for herself. "You're right" she replied, "but don't worry. It's nice and clean, and the musicians are fine." We stopped talking as the curtain rose and became absorbed with *The Bartered Bride.*

The shock came at intermission. The minute the lights were turned on a member of the orchestra motioned to me! His expression was displeasure. There was a disturbance among the players, and I sensed trouble ahead.

It only took one look to make me gasp! The floor of the pit was covered with about five inches of water. Those poor people had been playing Smetana's beautiful music with all its overture, arias, and choruses as if nothing was the matter.

I wanted to cry and run, but didn't. The maintenance man was called into action. He, too, was startled at the sight, and could only explain what had caused the disaster.

The auditorium was new, having been dedicated three months before. "Until now," he explained, "we have not had enough continual rain to discover this defect. There is a drainage outlet over in the corner. It evidently was not installed properly, and the water is backing up here, I can't do anything about it until tomorrow."

We apologized and apologized and asked forgiveness. The opera orchestra members were understanding. They tried not to cause a fuss and said, "The show must go on." The opera continued and the feet of the musicians had a good soaking. The depth of the water did not increase anymore after intermission. There were no hard feelings, and both students and audience were pleased with the production.

The following morning, Dr. Worthley kept his promise to sing a solo in our Episcopal Church. He was an inspiration to the choir and a treat to the congregation.

I am still singing in that choir and have been doing so for sixty-five years, some of the time serving as director. For that reason, I can appreciate what an effort it must have been for Maxwell Worthley to come out a Sunday morning to sing a solo after two opera performances.

Again it was our loyal friend, Miss Lily Peter, who made this opera possible. She provided the necessary funds to cover every expense including the contract fee and production costs for both performances.

Miss Lily's generosity was without parallel, ranging from feeding a baby chicken in a little cage in her bedroom to a big donation for the Medical Research Department at Vanderbilt University in Nashville, Tennessee. She has given to causes to educate young people, to save Big Creek from being channeled, to help the River Academy, and on and on.

As Poet Laureate of Arkansas, she was proud of our state and did not miss a chance to give it a boost, particularly so for education and the state universities. The money she gave away came from successful farming of 8,000 acres of land she inherited from her brother, Jesse Peter. Miss Lily could drive a truck or stay all night at her gin during her harvest season. As one writer put it, "What Miss Lily has given us all is a taste of culture—culture in the cotton fields."

She also loved Warfield Concerts and what they represented—culture, refinement, and classical music. By sponsoring *The Bartered Bride*, she helped the University and Warfield Concerts and gave the public an opportunity to come to an opera.

Betty Faust, a Warfield Committee member, and I decided that Miss Lily deserved to be honored with a Lily Peter Day in Phillips County. We worked together making arrangements and assuming responsibility for the whole event to take place on March 1, 1982.

Printed here is an article from the *Arkansas Democrat* which describes the schedule for the day:

HER STATE, HER COUNTY SALUTE MISS LILY PETER

A grand occasion for a grand lady.

It's Miss Lily Peter Day in Arkansas, so proclaimed by Gov. Frank White.

As a former pupil of Miss Lily, I received an invitation to the celebration in her home county of Phillips, but, alas, won't be able to go. *Democrat* brass prefer—nay, expect—the presence of the editor when the spring fashion section is being published.

But look what I'll miss:

Some time on noon a caravan will form to drive to Miss Lily's home near Marvell. They will drive Arkansas' poet laureate to Helena—West Helena where the motorcade will tour the city, giving the guest of honor plenty of time to see her many friends throughout the town and to view some of the changes she's had a hand in.

Later that evening a reception in her honor is scheduled at Phillips County Community College. She's to be in the receiving line to receive the loving congratulations of the admirers of this Marvell poet, farmer and lover of the arts.

Then there's to be a banquet, and Betty Faust, one of the planners said that letters from all over the world will be read praising this great lady.

Folks are coming from everywhere to offer their compliments in person—Reed Lewis of Elgin, Ill., who portrayed Father Marquette in the 1976 re-enactment of the Mississippi River journey of Joliet and Marquette; Dr. James Martin, chancellor of the University of Arkansas, Dr. Alexander Heard, chancellor of Vanderbilt University, Dr. John Ferguson, Arkansas Historical Commission, Dr. O.B. Emerson of the University of Alabama, and Dr. Rayburn Moore of the University of Georgia.

After the banquet a most fitting tribute—a free concert in the Lily Peter Auditorium at the college.

Helen Mosby, who is making arrangements for the music, said, "After all she's given us, it's only right that the people of this community should want to give her a concert in return."

Music will be by a string quintet from the Arkansas Symphony Orchestra.

My favorite Miss Lily story—and you've probably read it here before—concerns our conversation one day when we walked to school together.

Now when I was a student at Helena High School— which was a junior high as well—we didn't have busses to ride, and our parents thought 12-year-old feet could make the 7 or 8 blocks just fine.

So I'm tromping along when I meet up with my teacher.

Always one to investigate young minds, Miss Lily started talking about books. Now I made good grades under Miss Lily, and she thought I was a lot smarter than I was—or am.

"And whose works are you reading now, dear?" asked she.

Dumb kid—I told the truth. "Faith Baldwin."

And today I can't remember a single one of those "works."

But I did find—as many others who studied with Miss Lily—that there is memorable writing long remembered, romance that warms forever in the works of such as Charles Dickens.

Thank you, ma'am.

And have a happy Miss Lily Peter Day.

—Betty Woods February 23, 1982

At the banquet in her honor, Miss Lily was seated between Betty and me. We both knew that she reveled in making a gracious speech at a meeting or party, sometimes talking longer than time allowed.

All during dinner, we cautioned her to speak briefly because of the need to move on into the auditorium for the musical program.

She was welcomed, she was greeted, and she was complimented. Then her time came. Dressed in a blue chiffon gown, she stood up with her brightest smile and gracefully bowed saying, "Thank you, thank you, thank you!" She sat down! That was her speech. Cheers and bravos came from the guests as they rose and the dinner was over.

After Miss Lily died, the Wooten family who were the beneficiaries of her estate gave a concert in her memory on Monday, April 6, 1992. They appropriately chose the Arkansas Symphony Orchestra.

Inside the first page of the program was the following message:

A MEMORIAL CONCERT

This concert is presented in loving memory of Miss Lily Peter who died July 26, 1991, at the age of one hundred. It is graciously sponsored by her family— Michael and Sherry Wooten and their three children, Damon, Shawn and Kathryn. Knowing that her life was filed with the joy of music, they chose the Arkansas Symphony Orchestra for the occasion.

The Warfield Concerts Committee will be forever grateful for Miss Lily's continual support through the years. Every season she either completely sponsored a concert or joined with the committee in presenting one. We always welcomed her advice and her encouragement. She was our great benefactor, but most of all we loved her for the gentle kind person that she was.

Miss Lily's loyalty, her patriotism and her generosity have been without parallel. We feel sure that her spirit is with us tonight.

The Rabbi

A loss that was deeply felt by the whole community was the sudden death on the morning of September 22, 1977, of Rabbi Samuel R. Schillman, who had been the Rabbi at Temple Beth El in Helena for 18 years. Making the distressing news more poignant was the fact he was prepared to come to the Temple to begin the Yom Kippur services scheduled for that day. The services, nevertheless, did take place without delay with attorney David Solomon, a member of the congregation, taking charge.

I was in the choir the day the Rabbi died. Although we were shocked by such sad news, we sang with all our hearts to make it the best we could do. The music used at Temple Beth El was written by S. Schlesinger and is indescribably beautiful. The memorial service concluded with the anthem, "The Lord Will Give His Angels Charge Over Thee" and was as uplifting as anything I have ever heard.

There was one lone old-fashioned electric light bulb in the choir loft. Apparently it had been there for years, the clear glass showing the filaments when the light was turned on. It was used as a signal to the choir from Rabbi Schillman. When he turned on the light from the pulpit underneath the choir loft, we would know he was starting the service. During the sermon, three quick flashes by the light bulb meant he was ending his sermon and we must be ready with the next anthem. That September day we had no signals.

Rabbi Schillman was one of the first three appointers for the Warfield Concerts Committee. I was honored to be his choice for a member. I admired him and respected his judgment. We were good friends in a formal sort of way, always speaking to each other with dignity and politeness. We both liked the arts—particularly classical music.

In December 1967, I received a call from him asking me to come to his office. Wondering why, I soon found out. He had chosen me to be on the Warfield Concerts Committee with these instructions, "Do not worry about the size of the crowd. Offer music of high quality just as the S.D. Warfield will has instructed." His words have stayed with me until this day.

In addition to his rabbinical responsibilities, he believed in walking, not a little refreshing constitutional stroll or sauntering around before breakfast, but walking miles every day—more like a long hike. It was a serious matter to Rabbi Schillman. He could be found as far as ten miles from town briskly swinging his cane in rhythmical precision. He was known to walk over the Helena Bridge into Mississippi or south

of town near the cotton fields. He has truly been
missed, especially at the concerts to which he loyally
came as often as possible.

Of course we started talking about a suitable concert in memory of the Rabbi. Whether through luck,
determination, or negotiation or perhaps all three, we
found a perfect group, The National Choir of Israel.
Since the 1977-78 season was already settled, we were
able to make a contract with the Israelis for Thursday,
November 9, 1978.

Their American tour that year was limited and carefully planned. We were lucky to be one of the
approved places. In the cities, the choir was not per-
mitted to leave the hotels except for performances, but
in Helena, being a smaller town that was considered
quiet and peaceful, they were thrilled over walking
around outside to catch a glimpse of what it was like
in our river community.

Arriving late Wednesday afternoon at the Holiday
Inn, the foliage on the hills was resplendent in autumnal colors of red, yellow, purple, and gold and was
made even more brilliant by the red and gold of the
sun as it slipped below the horizon, an ideal setting to
warm the spirits of the travelers as they filed into the
motel. Nearly all of them spoke English, which helped
tremendously in welcoming them.

Since every Wednesday night we have choir practice at St. John's Church, I had a sudden thought. Why
not invite them to come? They were delighted! I

promised I would be back at seven-thirty to take as many as could pile into my car. They were excited to go out and my poor car was filled with layers of people.

Everyone had a good time. They sang for us, and we sang for them. I surprised them by singing in Hebrew some of the phrases I had learned during my years in the Holiday choir at temple Beth El. For me it was a night of fun.

The next morning Dennis Burton, choral director at Central High School and a member of our choir at St. John's, took all of the Choir of Israel to his class, a nice experience for both his students and the choir.

Their concert that night was a highly creditable performance displaying a blend of well-trained voices singing their best. After the concert, Mrs. David Solomon entertained the singers with a supper party just for the Choir at the Holiday Inn. From all reports, everyone was hungry and eagerly consumed our American food.

For two years after that, I had notes from several of the members saying, "We will always remember your friendly town."

Philippe Entremont

The sight of the shining black Bosendorfer—a nine-foot concert grand piano with five more keys extending from the bass clef than has the Steinway or Baldwin of similar size—was a thrill to behold. Polished to mirror-like perfection, it had been placed on the S.D. Warfield stage ready for the program to start.

The date was January 26, 1980. The eighteen member Vienna Chamber Orchestra with the celebrated pianist Philippe Entremont as guest artist and conductor was performing.

Traveling with their own Bosendorfer was extremely helpful to the Warfield Committee. We were relieved of the responsibility of having a piano serviced and tuned to exactly the right pitch for the instruments. Also, those who were there that night had the pleasure of hearing a super excellent artist playing a Bosendorfer, a piano which a majority of them had never seen or heard.

It was fascinating to watch Mr. Entremont as he executed the difficult piano passages and at the same time directed the dynamics of the instrumentalists with a perfect blend of piano and strings. The Mozart cadenzas flowed from his fingertips and the Strauss waltzes and polkas took our minds to Vienna, that beautiful city of dreams.

According to Musical America's International Directory and ICM Artists' Management, Philippe Entremont is (now sixteen years later) still with the Vienna Chamber Orchestra and also principal conductor of the Netherlands Chamber Orchestra.

No Thank You

The clock in the kitchen showed fifteen minutes after six. Mary in her fresh white uniform glanced at the rolls. "Looking good," she said, "and everything else will soon be ready." For twenty years, Mary had been making rolls and cooking meals in that kitchen. She liked to do the little "extras" that were necessary for parties. Louis, who regularly took care of the neighborhood yards, was there too in his white coat to serve and keep things going in the dining room. I felt confident about the evening.

I decided to take a last look in there. The table, covered with a long white damask linen cloth, was well-set with my best French Haviland china and Francis I silver, service plates, bread and butter plates, and of course the cut glass goblets; everything was in order down to the last little after-dinner coffee spoons.

It was January 11, 1984, so soon after Christmas that I had cut my poinsettia blooms from their pots and used them to make a lovely arrangement in a silver bowl for the centerpiece. The effect was quite festive. The guests were expected at 7:00 P.M.

The honorees were to be Byron Janis and his wife, Maria Cooper Janis. He was our Warfield Series pianist scheduled to give a concert the following night, and she was the glamorous daughter of the famous actor, Gary Cooper. She was slim and tall and very much resembled her father, particularly in her eyes.

The other guests were the Warfield Committee members—at that date being Betty Faust, Helen Benton, and Cassie Brothers—and their husbands, and Katherine Hill, the concert coordinator. We had decided to wear our best evening clothes for such a special occasion. Maria and Byron would certainly expect nothing less. There was no doubt, the thought of Maria Cooper in our midst created a flurry of excitement, enough to inspire the committee to arrive early.

There we stood, in front of the fireplace where the logs blazed with a force that seemed to defy the cold winter night. The heat felt good. To me, a cheerful fire does as much for a party as flowers.

The doorbell rang. Mr. and Mrs. Byron Janis were warmly received as was Katherine Hill, who was in charge of their transportation. Maria removed her long mink coat. She was wearing a very simple dark knee-length dress, a contrast to our party clothes, but she wore it with style, and, as my mother used to say to me, "Simplicity can be elegant." With Byron in his conservative black suit, they were indeed an elegant pair.

Since they replied, "No thank you," to a glass of

wine or any other form of alcohol, we were soon seated for dinner, Maria at my right, and Byron at my left. I enjoyed being able to talk with them, but was very disappointed when again they said, "No thank you," to a slice of the juicy beef roast. "We do not eat meat of any kind," Maria told me. I comforted myself with the thought that the vegetables were good and we had a fruit salad.

Trying to make our honorees feel at ease, we exerted ourselves to talk about music and Hollywood. That proved successful until time for dessert. Louis cleared the table of dishes; in grand style he removed all crumbs with the silent butler, and then brought in a large bowl of chocolate icebox dessert covered with whipped cream. If anything could be enticing, this surely was. To Maria and Byron it was not tempting, and for the third time I heard the words, "No thank you. We do not eat dessert."

Nevertheless, we laughed and talked for a while before everyone left. The fire had turned to ashes and the house began to be cool. For me, I felt happy that the night had come to an end.

The next day Helen Benton gave a beautiful luncheon for Maria, who excused herself shortly after we finished eating to go to the auditorium with Byron while he practiced. He suffered with back pains and wore a brace during the entire time he was here. She was aware of his discomfort and tried to help him as much as possible.

In spite of the back brace, his concert was extremely good. The audience was very appreciative and generous with applause. He was a great artist.

Cassie and Bill Brothers entertained with a party after the concert. The Janises were most gracious, responding pleasantly to much of the conversation.

Betty Faust drove them to the airport the next morning. Afterward she called me to say she was back. "We crossed the bridge [Mississippi River] and took a short cut through Lula."

The town of Lula could be described as the remains of a once busy farming center. The use of machines such as tillers, cotton pickers, and combines in the production of cotton and soybeans had destroyed activity in Lula, leaving only a little worn out country store, a post office, a few small vacant frame buildings, and a railroad track that was used for freight cars.

Many other little communities in the Mississippi River Delta had suffered the same fate as Lula because of mechanization in farming.

Betty continued, "As we drove through Lula, Byron remarked, 'What an interesting movie set. We often see these in Hollywood.' I did not want to disillusion them but just had to confess that he was looking at one of our former farming centers."

That was the last we saw or heard of Byron and Maria except for one time shortly after they were here when I happened to see him on the Johnny Carson show making beautiful music.

No Luggage

Tuesday, January 27, 1981, 2 P.M. The telephone rang. It was Katherine Hill calling from the Memphis Airport where she was meeting pianist Tedd Joselon. He was scheduled to give a concert in Helena that night for a fee of $1,750.

She broke the news gently, "We're in a little trouble," she said. "Tedd is here but his luggage was not on the plane. His dress clothes are in the luggage and we have been told there is no chance of having it before tomorrow."

"Oh! What can we do!" my thoughts began to race finally deciding to tell her, "Don't worry. I'll call around and find a tuxedo from someone his size. That is all I can think of. It surely isn't tails and white tie but certainly would be better than his traveling clothes."

My search began. We needed a tux to fit a person 5'9" weighing 165 pounds. After several unsuccessful calls, I reached Vic Juengle, a prominent Helena business man and Chief Executive Officer of Juengle Associates, Insurance and Investments. He had exactly the right tuxedo and very kindly agreed to let us use it. His wife, Janet, has also been most successful in the business world as owner of Juengle Interior Designs. Her reputation for beauty and creativity is recognized throughout the Mid-South.

By the time Katherine and Tedd arrived, this most needed garment was in my hands—tux, freshly pressed and laundered shirt, black tie, and socks. It was not the best fit in the world, but he could wear it. He would have to use his own shoes which fortunately were black.

We frequently housed our artists, sometimes entertaining them in our own homes or asking friends to help. For free accommodations they would reduce their charge. Cassie and Bill Brothers had generously provided for Tedd Joselon their guest house with an indoor swimming pool. He was much impressed to have such a spacious place to stay. He found the pool refreshing and said water did wonders for his hands.

His concert was sensational. He played with a certain intensity that is hard to describe, particularly as his crescendos come forth with such force, almost breathtaking. It has been said about Tedd that "He dared to attempt the impossible, but always succeeded." After hearing him perform, I can understand why.

He had impressed everybody to the extent that we invited him back for the following year on January 19, 1982. For a change, he brought his friend Roger Press to join him in the performance, *Four Hands on the Keyboard.* (This time he arrived with a well-packed suitcase.) It was an enjoyable concert, but the contrast in their talents was too obvious.

Tedd and I became friends. For several years, I had notes from him. He did not seem to care much about publicity or his financial needs. He just loved to play the piano and the opportunity to perform. Now I think he spends nearly all his time in Europe.

Katherine Hill

After the death of Bessie McGee in May 1974, Katherine Stephens Hill became our concert coordinator for the next twelve years. She was excellent in that position, having lived in Helena all of her life. Her three children, Herbert Jr., Johnnye June, and Mary, were grown, but as children, they lived here in their antebellum home, Estevan Hall, built in 1826. It was occupied by the United States Army during the Civil War.

The grounds surrounding this historic white frame home are filled with ancient magnolia trees. During warm months their huge white flowers are a sight to behold. A heavy black wrought-iron gate opens on a long brick walkway leading to the tall row of wide steps joining the veranda, which extends across the front of the house. Seven white columns add another distinctive feature of southern charm.

The foundation like those on Ohio Street mentioned in the first chapter is high above the ground to protect against flooding by the unpredictable Mississippi. From the veranda, a wide view of the river could be seen in the distance. (Now that refreshing site is ruined by commercial buildings.)

Estevan Hall has been well cared for and is considered a tourist attraction. Katherine has enjoyed taking visitors or tourist groups through it as she tells them interesting stories about the past.

Katherine Hill, a member of the First Methodist Church, was a civic leader with many loyal friends. She had great pride in our community. We frequently talked about the concerts, fortunately being able to see a humorous side to difficult situations. No matter how carefully we planned, something unforeseen always happened. The upset might be good or bad, but whatever it was, Katherine seemed to know exactly what to do and could quietly and efficiently settle the surprise dilemma.

I remember one time she had to rush home to cook a steak at four in the afternoon for an opera singer that just had to have beef in the afternoon in order to sing well at night.

Another incident involved a couple from out-of-town with a four month old baby. They had driven an hour and a half to the concert, but she was forced to tell them that no one under six years of age was allowed in the auditorium. They turned around and drove home.

A member of a foreign choral group had an annoying sore throat. Katherine took him to see Doctor Alfred Berger who gave him a treatment and some medicine to relieve his discomfort. To the amazement, of his patient, Doctor Berger said, "No charge!" The young singer in his limited English and European accent thanked him with a big smile and said, "America, nice!"

There were often calls to mend a costume or press evening gowns. On one occasion, two women ironed for several hours on ballet wardrobes.

Always, orange juice, cold drinks, and snacks were available behind the scenes for those who needed refreshing. For every concert, Katherine wore a long evening dress. She felt it gave it her respect and made her easier to be identified.

I am sorry to relate that she died on Friday, April 29, 1994. I lost a dear friend, but she left a wonderful memory for us all.

When Katherine Hill resigned in the fall of 1985, Maureen Jones succeeded her as concert coordinator. This position was becoming more and more demanding including production, publicity, and programs.

Maureen accepted the challenge, a tremendous task for a newcomer, but Maureen proved herself indispensable in the following years. She had a keen knowledge of the theater and a fine taste for good music. She also had initiative and energy.

She and her husband, Neville, and two children, Ashley and Virginia, moved here from Liverpool, England, in 1982 when Neville took over the management of the NORAC Company. Soon Maureen was asked to be secretary of St. John's Episcopal Church, and Neville was welcomed as a choir member. The Reverend Duane Saba was the Rector of St. John's at the time.

Their children are grown now. Virginia is studying voice and drama in New York City, and Ashley is working in Columbia, Missouri.

Lorin Hollander

Over the years Warfield Audiences heard many more brilliant pianists. They were all accomplished masters of the keyboard, and their program choices were superb. It would be impossible to single out any particular one as the best. I just enjoyed each concert as long as it lasted.

A great favorite with the Memphis Symphony Orchestra and seven times their guest artist was pianist Lorin Hollander. He made a host of friends in that Bluff City and felt very much at home, sometimes adding a few surprises to his performance. I happened to be there one time when he walked out to play, wearing cowboy boots and a plaid shirt. The audience apparently liked his novel appearance and seemed to be stimulated to more than the usual applause.

Lorin Hollander played on the Warfield Series on January 17, 1977, but for us he wore the traditional white tie and tails. That delightful concert was well attended. There was a large number of out-of-town visitors, including Maestro Vincent de Frank of the Memphis Symphony Orchestra and a group of distinguished Memphians.

Mr. Hollander arrived in town the day before the performance. He immediately wanted to practice. Since the auditorium was in use, he came to my home and used my Baldwin baby grand.

When the two-hour drilling of scales, chords, arpeggios, and trills was over, I walked in the room carrying an ice pick in my hand. He looked up with amazement, maybe even with alarm. Perhaps he considered it a weapon until I handed it to him saying, "Would you please scratch your name on the back of the music rack."

The idea had come to me while Lorin was practicing, a most unusual way to acquire autographs. "Well," he commented as he carefully blocked out LORIN HOLLANDER in rather jagged letters, "I have always wanted to give a piano a big kick, and maybe this little act will satisfy that wild emotion." We both laughed. Little did he realize (neither did I) that his bold autograph was the first of more names to be marked on my piano.

Through the years, any of the Warfield artists who had been in my home were presented with the ice pick to carve an autograph on the piano. Some of those who are represented there are: Sherrill Milnes and his accompanist, Jon Spong, Gilda Cruz Roma, Eugene Istomin, Fred Waring, Byron Janis, Roberta Peters, Boris Goldovsky, Cristine Coates, and numerous others.

A reception at my house followed the Hollander recital, but the many guests had only a short time to visit with the honoree. At about eleven, snow began to fall. Everyone hurriedly said good night and rushed away to drive home before the streets were covered.

Maureen Jones

Through Warfield Concerts and the Episcopal Church, Maureen Jones has become my valued friend. I have asked her to briefly describe her emotional stress over leaving her homeland in England to live in a new country:

JULY 17, 1982—Neville met the children and me at Memphis Airport about 4:00 P.M., and we drove down Highway 61 toward our new home in Helena, Arkansas. As I looked out over field after field of cotton and soy beans, I kept thinking, "Surely we will come to a town soon." After a while, we did, going through Tunica, Mississippi, a rather lifeless little place. I later learned that Tunica County had been described by newspaper columnists as one of the poorest places in the country. I can certainly agree with them.

We saw deserted shacks (Southerners call them shot-gun houses) not fit for habitation. Many were in the middle of fields where they had been left to fall in. There was an empty store by the side of the road with two gray-haired men sitting on the porch doing nothing.

If we had been moving to a third world country, I would not have been surprised, but this was the United

States of America, one of the richest countries in the world. We soon left 61 with a right turn that took us to a bridge over the Mississippi River into Helena and a new life.

During the next two weeks I was very busy putting our home together, getting our children settled and trying to make comparisons of all the unfamiliar labels at the grocery store and the strange money I had in my billfold.

By that time I had also come to realize that entertainment was very limited with only one movie house in the town. I began to feel resentful that I was so far removed from the rich source of culture that had been such an important part of my life in England.

One evening my husband came home and announced that there was a Warfield Concert that night. I did not know what to expect, but we decided to go and it was wonderful. I had found an oasis in this cultural desert. That evening changed my perspective of Helena. Now I had something to look forward to every few weeks that was close to home. Now I felt I had a life and my children would not grow up uneducated in the arts.

Neville and Maureen bought a house in Waverly Wood, an attractive wooded residential area between Helena and West Helena. They proceeded to give it a touch of the English countryside by adding window boxes of bright colored flowers. Neville's "green thumb" keeps them flourishing. Every year when the warm weather comes, I look forward to the boxes and any new specimens growing in them.

The Joneses were quick to enter into the spirit of the town. They gladly took civic responsibilities and fulfilled social obligations. They have a real place in the community, and we "old-timers" feel lucky that they have made Helena their home.

Maureen enjoyed the friendships she made with some of our pianists. One of her favorites was Eugene Graf of Charleston, South Carolina. His Helena appearance was on Thursday, April 30, 1992. The next morning, he conducted a Master Class followed by a youth concert in the early afternoon.

He was a very nice looking polite young man, generous with his talent and friendly. Maureen found him appreciative and easy to work with.

In contrast, the highly recognized pianist Misha Dichter performed here on May 1, 1986, without ever really talking to anyone. He arrived in his car just shortly before the concert was to begin.

Immediately, he went to his dressing room until time to appear on the stage that Watson's Florist had most elegantly decorated (a service they often gave to Warfield Concerts). At each side of the stage stood large wicker baskets of white flowers and greenery. These were further enhanced by potted plants banked around them. A garland of green foliage framed the front edge of the stage floor with tiny lights sparkling through the leaves. The S.D. Warfield Stage was indeed arrayed in finery.

I doubt if Misha Dichter ever saw any of our decorations. As the lights dimmed, he went straight to the piano and played a perfectly beautiful program. Without a single encore, he walked off going directly to his automobile and drove away. That was the last we ever saw or heard of Misha Dichter. His bill for the performance was $5,000.

Maureen took good care of Jose Carlos Cocorelli, a silver medalist in the most recent Van Cliburn International Piano Competition. Taking place every four years, it is one of the most influential in the "high-stakes piano world."

It was fascinating to hear Cocorelli tell of the months of intense concentration, practice, self-discipline, and determination required to reach the finals of such a prestigious event. In addition to the hours and hours of practice, a certain diet, exercise, and enough sleep were necessary for his achievement. He had continued to keep his strict routine.

Maureen brought him exactly the food he wanted: grilled chicken, dry toast, and skim milk. He loved dogs so she took him to her house to run around in the yard (for exercise) with her husband Neville's two golden retrievers. It happened to be April 25, 1991, one of those bright spring days in the Mississippi Delta when sunshine gives a special glow to the early green leaves and flowering shrubs, a day weather watchers like to refer to as a jewel.

He enjoyed the dogs but did not dare touch one for

fear of having a finger snapped by the friendly canines. Just a little nip on a hand could have a serious effect on his career. After having his diet food and the little outing, he returned to his room at the Edwardian Inn to relax before going to the auditorium to play one of the most delightful solo recitals I have ever heard. Cocorelli's superlative talent supported with self-discipline and determination surely makes him destined for greatness.

Chrissie

Dashing around Waverly Wood Drive on her bicycle, long golden red pigtails waving in the air, Mike, the German Shepard trotting loyally behind, that was Chrissie when I first knew her. Even then she had a forcefulness in her movements and a sparkle in her blue eyes that reflected spirit and determination. In later years, her cheerful energy gave others a feeling of well-being.

She is the daughter of Christine and Austin Coates, a prominent local attorney. Her mother, one of my dearest lifelong friends, is also known as Chrissie, and her father we called Big A. Big A himself, an originator of nicknames, had one for each of his children.

He called Mary Catherine, the oldest, Sweets. Then Austin Jr. became Monkeyman, and Chrissie, the youngest, acquired the title of Pigsey, the inspiration being her pigtails and assuredly not, as one might suppose, that wallowing barnyard animal executed in the cold of winter for sausage and fresh pork hams.

Such remarks take me back to the early thirties (a newlywed as Mrs. Cadwallader Leonidas Polk Jr.) and those stingy days of the Great Depression. I looked forward to "hog killing time"; from the country farms came fresh bacon, ribs, and hams, as well as lard (I shudder to think of the amount of cholesterol therein) rendered from their excessive fat; the refrigerator bulged with food for Thanksgiving and Christmas.

With apologies to Christine Coates Miller and Samuel Drake Warfield for straying off my subject with inappropriate remarks, I return to Chrissie at age four. On her own volition she left her friends and their outdoor activities for brief periods to come inside and play by ear pretty little tunes on the piano. Music lessons followed, and I had the pleasure of watching her develop her talent.

She loved all music even to the point of naming her horse Tristan after Richard Wagner's opera *Tristan and Isolde*. During parties she could be found seated at the piano playing whatever piece the crowd wanted to hear.

Christine Coates Miller is one of my favorite concert pianists. I have asked her to write the following article disclosing her experiences with Warfield Concerts and her friendship with S.D. Warfield:

> Behind every aspiring musician there are family, friends, teachers and a community that give help, support, and encouragement that nurture the artistic gift until it can take wing and fly on its own. This was never so clear to me as it was in my third appearance on the Warfield Concert Series where there were many people

in the audience who have been in my musical corner since I was a young person growing up in Helena.

Music was always a natural and integral part of my home life. Friends and neighbors dropping by our Waverly Wood home would inevitably gather around the piano to sing the old songs from the red books. "The Church In the Wildwood" and "When You and I Were Young Maggie" were favorites. Evenings were never complete until my cousin Jux sang "Old Man River," and Miss Bessie Tappan Jones her rendition of "Trees." Christmastime was especially festive and filled with music. My family always held open house on Christmas afternoon and my first recollection of S.D. Warfield dates from this time. S.D. loved a party and was a wonderful guest. He would arrive in a festive mood, his head crowned with a holly wreath and request I play Lecuona's "Maleguena" on the piano while he improvised an impromptu Spanish dance to the rhythmic strains of the music.

Significantly, and little known to me at the time, S.D., posthumously through his legacy, would become one of my major benefactors, not only by my appearances on the Warfield Concert Series but through the committee members like Helen Mosby, whose devoted service to the Warfield Series helped put Helena on the nation's concert map. In her long stint as an administrator, booking artists and promoting events, she acquired the skill of an entrepreneur and shared this experience generously with fledgling artists like myself, who were eager to make their way in the concert business.

The first professional engagement of my career came on November 2, 1969, several years after my graduation from college. The Warfield Concert Series was just beginning and a group of Arkansas musicians performed together in the Central High School Gym to a large and enthusiastic audience. I recall that everyone backstage had the performance jitters. Ben Selman, a fellow pianist from Little Rock, sat in a corner with his hands in a muff attempting to keep them warm until he went on stage. Even Bob Evans, the seasoned professional among us, paced back and forth, intent on keeping his focus and oblivious to the goings on around him. My own nervousness had not been helped by my father who innocently enough kept asking me all day if I was ready and did I know my music. The concert honored Miss Lily Peter, State Music Chairman for the Arkansas Territorial Sesquicentennial, and herself a loyal supporter of the arts. Miss Lily's eloquent opening remarks were followed by excellent performances from each of the musicians. It seemed fitting that so many of the performers were friends of S.D.

In 1973 I was invited to play a solo recital in the new Lily Peter Auditorium. The committee had recently purchased a magnificent Steinway Concert Grand. I remember when I first entered the beautiful hall with its perfect acoustics and saw the new piano on stage, I thought this could be New York, Chicago, any musical center, the surroundings were so elegant. The recital took place just a year after my debut at New York's Town Hall. Both events were major highs in my career. At the Helena concert, Mayor Kelly gave me a key to the city, bouquets of flowers were presented and as a tribute to S.D. and all that he had done for us, my final piece was "Maleguena." It seemed as though everything had come full circle.

One of the loves of my career has been a long musical affair with the works of Louis Moreau Gottschalk. Gottschalk (1829-69), a native of New Orleans, was the first American to win international acclaim as a composer, concert artist and cultural ambassador. In Gottschalk I feel a deep connection with my southern roots and my musical heritage from Phillips County. I know S.D. would have loved the music of Gottschalk too, as they both shared the spirit of the nineteenth century romantic. I was honored that the committee invited me to present my multimedia recital "Gottschalk, The Man and His Music," on the Warfield Music Festival May 3, 1996.

Another joy of my childhood was Helena's Civic Music concerts. My friends and I would rush to get a seat on the front row so we could be the first backstage after the concert to get the artist's autograph. Years later, in an old scrapbook, I found a program signed by the renowned American pianist John Browning, who played a recital in Helena at the very beginning of his career. I don't recall the performance, but I do remember the vivid impression Civic Music concerts made on my growing musical awareness. These artists were role models who introduced great music to a developing mind and fired my imagination with the possibility of becoming like them. It is speculated that S.D. adopted the concept of Civic Music in setting up the Warfield Foundation. In carrying on the tradition, his vision has brought the performances of the great and near great to Phillips County, benefitted artists like myself and insured that the cultural life of our community would be enriched for generations to come.

Chrissie, now 61, continues to have goals and accept challenges. Her energy and ambitions remain undiluted. A disciplined lifestyle has enabled her to achieve many of her objectives. I wish her the best in the years to come.

Happy Birthday

All the pianists we have had added superior quality to the series. One whom I shall always remember was Michael Boriskin, a native New Yorker. He opened the 1990-91 season with a thrilling concert on October 1, 1990.

We were introduced to Michael through Mrs. Miriam Solomon whose husband, David, was the attorney for the S.D. Warfield Estate. Mrs. Solomon, a friend of the Boriskin family, was familiar with Michael's extensive and successful concertizing around the world. She recommended him for a Warfield Concert. We appreciated her interest for what was a delightful occasion.

Award winning pianist Michael Boriskin will perform Monday, October 1, in Lily Peter Auditorium when the Warfield Concert Series opens a brand new season.

Through his many acclaimed recordings and performances, Boriskin has been recognized both here and abroad as a compelling and versatile interpreter of a widely varied repertoire. He has performed at many of the world's foremost concert venues including the Kennedy Center, the Lincoln Center, Carnegie Hall, BBC in London, RIAS Berlin, Theatre des Champs-Elysees in Paris, and the New York International Festival of Arts.

—*Daily World*
September 24, 1990

With such a schedule as this it would appear that Michael could do nothing but practice and perform. But I found him to be, in simple words, an all-around person.

He was comfortable with sports, politics, or history. Whatever the subject, Michael was informed, and his presence at a party created spirited conversation.

Unexpectedly, I was added to his program. He happened to find out that October 1 is my birthday (I have had many of them). His sharp brown eyes twinkled as he announced an encore. Sitting down he played "Happy Birthday, Helen Mosby." Thank you Michael Boriskin.

Traveling by Truck

Through my friendship with Martha J. Coleman, his personal representative, the Warfield committee was able to negotiate a contract with America's Virtuoso Pianist, Eugene Istomin, for a concert in Helena on January 19, 1993. We were most fortunate in the final agreement which included a fee of only $5,000—much less than he received in other places.

At age 67 Mr. Istomin had given more than 3,000 concerts in virtually every part of the world. To standing ovations in cities both large and small he has offered masterpieces of the romantic and classical repertoire. *The Washington Post* had called him an "International Treasure." The number of his consecutive solo recital and orchestral appearances has been absolutely unprecedented.

Today many artists bypass small communities in favor of the big cities. But Eugene Istomin told me, "It is important to reach out to the people who have less opportunity to enjoy the arts. I like these smaller places and the warmth and friendliness that prevails there."

The first Warfield Concerts Committee Left-to-right (Seated):
Helen Clopton Polk Mosby, Sam Anderson, and Rosalind Solomon;
(Standing) Appointments Committee. Left to Right: Mayor Bill
Stratton, Rabbi Schillman, the Reverend Phil Leach, and Attorney
David Solomon.

Miss Lily Peter and Carlos Smith at the ground breaking for the Fine Arts Center.

Christine Coates Miller made her debut at New York's Town Hall and was a finalist in the First International Gottschalk Competition.

Sherrill Milnes as Don Giovanni.

Arthur Fiedler of the Boston Pops.

WARFIELD FOUNDATION CONCERTS

PRESENTS

THE MEMPHIS SYMPHONY

ORCHESTRA in CONCERT

With Violinist

YOUNG UCK KIM

as Guest Artist

MONDAY APRIL 22, 1968

AT

Central High Gymnasium

8 P.M.

ADMISSION FREE

The first concert poster, 1968.

Miss Lily Peter takes a bow at the dedication program. Left to right: Mrs. Fred Faust, Helen Mosby, Miss Lily Peter, Senator John McClellan.

Miss Lily Peter and Van Cliburn on the stage of the Lily Peter Auditorium.

Pianist Eugene Istomin, who shipped his two Steinways by truck, autographed my piano with an ice pick.

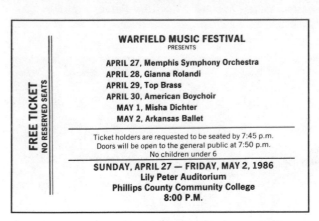

WARFIELD MUSIC FESTIVAL
PRESENTS

APRIL 27, Memphis Symphony Orchestra
APRIL 28, Gianna Rolandi
APRIL 29, Top Brass
APRIL 30, American Boychoir
MAY 1, Misha Dichter
MAY 2, Arkansas Ballet

Ticket holders are requested to be seated by 7:45 p.m.
Doors will be open to the general public at 7:50 p.m.
No children under 6

SUNDAY, APRIL 27 — FRIDAY, MAY 2, 1986
Lily Peter Auditorium
Phillips County Community College
8:00 P.M.

FREE TICKET
NO RESERVED SEATS

A ticket to the Warfield Music Festival (1986).

The New York City Opera National Company's Rigoletto included Robert McFarland as Rigoletto (back), Joyce Guyer as Gilda, and Michael Sylvester as Duke of Mantua. Photo by Susan Cook of Martha Swope Associates.

The Committee for the Music Festival (clockwise from top left): Cassie Brothers, Betty Faust, Helen Benton, Helen Mosby.

Miss Lily Peter and Helen Mosby in the living room of the Mosby home.

A reception at the Mosby home followed the dedication of the Lily Peter Auditorium and the Fine Arts Center. Seated at the table are Mrs. Fred Faust (left) and Mrs. Tom Choate (right).

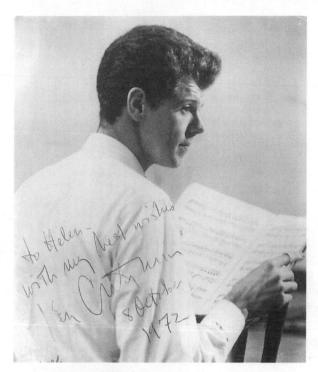

Van Cliburn, 1972.

Roberta Peters at the time of her appearance in the Warfield Series.

The Vienna Chamber Orchestra, Philippe Entremont, Conductor and Piano Soloist.

Artist's rendering of the Fine Arts Center and the Lily Peter Auditorium.

Joy Brown Wiener, Concert Master of the Memphis Symphony Orchestra.

Helen Mosby and Warfield Committee member Betty Hendrix at a reception at the Phillips County Community College.

Boris Goldovsky, "Mr. Opera." Courtesy Herbert Barrett Management.

Cadet Glee Club of the United States Military Academy, officers and Officer in Charge, 1969.

Vienna Choir Boys, March 1983.

Free Ticket

Warfield Foundation Concerts
Presents
The Roger Wagner Chorale

Tuesday, November 19, 1968
8 P. M.
Central Junior High Gymnasium

SECT. 1   Row................   Seat...............

Free Ticket

Warfield Foundation Concerts
Presents
Harry James and his Orchestra
In Concert

Monday Night, April 21, 1969
8:00 P. M.
Central High School Gymnasium

SECT. 2   Row................   Seat................

Tickets to two of the Warfield Concert Series events held in the Central High School Gymnasium prior to the opening of the Fine Arts Center.

In the grand old manner of great artists, Mr.
Istomin traveled to Helena. He brought his two nine-
foot Steinway Concert grand pianos and a technician
with him. The technician was an attractive, highly educated lady, not in the least like someone expected to
work on a piano, but in conversing with her, I realized
there was nothing that she did not know about a keyboard instrument. She even examined our own
Steinway and gave us some good advice about a few
problems we were having with it.

First to arrive was the huge black GMC top kick
truck supplied by General Motors with simple gold
lettering EUGENE ISTOMIN PIANIST. Although it was
only a truck, to me it was impressive because I knew
what was inside. I was glad to be assured by the driver
that the two Steinways had made the trip in perfect
condition.

Mr. Istomin soon came along in his private automobile with the lady technician who would be tuning
one of the pianos as quickly as it was placed on the
stage. Again, I asked a question, "Do you ever ride in
the truck?" He readily explained to me that now and
then he did enjoy riding in the truck if the distance was
not too far. He found it was rather nice to have a little
break from the monotony of the car.

He gave a magnificent performance to a crowd that
was not as large as usual, but their enthusiasm and
appreciation for the wonderful music made up for any
lack of numbers.

According to the review in our *Daily World*, several "were present to hear what must have been one of the true artistic highlights of the auditorium's history."

The concert was followed by a reception at my house. I was happy to have a chance to give him the ice pick to scratch his name on my piano.

In addition to being one of the world's greatest musicians, Eugene Istomin was an attractive gentleman. I will always value the memory of having him in my home.

Roberta

April 13, 1977. Dressed in a new spring print, navy blue and white with a red belt, I stood at the Memphis Airport awaiting the arrival of the fair Roberta. Others were there meeting friends or relatives, but none, I'm sure, as elated as I. How privileged I was to be greeting the enchanting diva of the Metropolitan Opera Company, the world famous soprano, Roberta Peters. Tingling with expectation my heart was skipping around and my blood pressure must surely have been on an upward swing. The officer in charge was unlocking the gate.

For several days, my thoughts had been trying to settle on the appropriate salutation for our meeting. "How was your trip?" seemed too dull for words as did "I'm happy to see you," another worn-out phrase. So, "Greetings from the Warfield Committee," seemed better.

A little inner voice told me to calm down and to be patient, or I might not be able to think.

She should surely be pleased to hear that my good friend, Virginia Straub, was having a little supper party in her garden and that I would love to take her there as soon as we reached Helena. Well that idea was doomed to become extinct.

The gate opened and there stood Roberta wearing a stunning red suit trimmed with brass buttons and a red and white blouse, a perfect compliment to her black hair and deep blue eyes with their delicately arched eyebrows. Her appearance was a delight to the beholder.

To my surprise she had a companion, a pleasant lady having more years to her credit than Roberta, who quietly and efficiently took care of all traveling responsibilities. This sensible arrangement allowed Roberta to conserve her energy and relax before singing the following night. I found her companion friendly and interesting to talk with, but I cannot recall her name.

Miss Peters was familiar with Memphis, of being there when the Metropolitan Opera company made annual tours in the spring stopping at Atlanta, Memphis, and Dallas. Since those days, the development of excellent regional opera companies and the ever rising cost of production have put an end of touring of the Metropolitan Opera Company. She had fond memories of the lavish parties after the opera given for the cast at Justine's, a most elite and sophisticated restaurant where guests were royally treated to the South's finest cuisine. These extravagant affairs were noted for their gaiety, toasting, singing, and joking; the stars of the operatic world would cut loose, shedding all restraint and join in the fun and merrymaking. Naturally, Roberta had in the back of her mind dinner at Justine's, but it was only six, a somewhat early hour to dine.

After speaking agreeably for several minutes, I extended my invitation to Virginia's supper. She was quick to exclaim, "Oh no, we must go to Justine's!" I weakly mentioned, "If we stay here for dinner we will have to drive in darkness the remainder of the way." "I'll be glad to drive in darkness," replied our beautiful soprano. The discussion ended. We would go to Justine's.

I was embarrassed to tell her I did not know the way to that exclusive restaurant. Making a flimsy excuse to stop a moment, I ran in the airport hotel and called Justine's, asking explicit instructions for driving there. The result: I drove straight to the door and parked right in front of it. There was not one person having dinner. We were courteously treated as strangers. I was sorry because I knew Roberta was disappointed, but we had a nice meal and then continued on our journey on Highway 61, over the Helena bridge, and to the Holiday Inn.

I immensely enjoyed our conversation during the one and a half hour drive from Memphis. We talked seriously about singing (a subject I never tire of discussing) and the strict schedule necessary to stay in condition. I finally worked myself into enough courage to tell her I sang in St. John's Episcopal choir and also had sung many years in the holiday choir at Temple Beth El. Roberta confessed to owning one hundred gowns in her performing wardrobe. I wondered which one she would choose for her solo recital the following night.

Her selection was an exquisite pink one, which gave the effect of floating as she came out on the stage. The ladies of my mother's generation would have called her "a vision of loveliness." She was indeed all of that and more when, accompanied by David Benedict, she began to sing.

Her glorious voice, both lyric and coloratura, gave the listeners a thrill. Pure effortless high C's floated in the air. The crowning glory of the evening took the audience to Vienna, the city of dreams, with her rendition of Viljia from the *Merry Widow* by Franz Lehar. Roberta loved that song and we loved her for singing it.

Following the recital, a light reception for a limited number of guests was held at my home. (Roberta had requested nothing elaborate.) She was genuinely cordial to everyone. When we said good-bye at my front door, she put into my arms a big Thank You, a large bouquet of red roses she had received on stage. For me, it was in the words of the American song writer Carrie Jacobs Bond (1862-1946), "the end of a Perfect Day."

In the December 1981 issue of *Ovation Magazine*

(no longer being published), I read a story written by Ivan Berger about Roberta Peters. In it she tells of singing in opera houses around the world:

> Vienna was one of my very favorites. If they love you, it's most exciting. But if they don't love you, well, I have heard terrible, terrible stories of their spitting on a tenor when he came out the stage door. They love opera, they breathe it, they eat it. The chambermaids in the hotel know how the performance was the night before. I have very, very happy memories of it.

Her debut at the Metropolitan Opera House came very suddenly at the tender age of 19. She was called in to sing the role of Zerlina in *Don Giovanni* replacing Nadina Conner who had become ill. She was a tremendous success. Roberta Peters became a star.

Roberta came back to Helena as guest soloist with the Arkansas Symphony Orchestra on Sunday, October 23, 1983. The program—*A Night in Vienna*.

On this occasion, I had the pleasure of having her as an overnight guest in my home. No reception this time, only a chicken dinner in my dining room after the concert. We were joined by Betty Faust and Laura Deitz, who was the feature editor for the local paper, *The Helena-West Helena World*. She had a brief interview with Laura and then went off to bed in my guestroom. I will have to confess that I had washed curtains and invested in new lace-trimmed sheets and pillowcases for the antique mahogany four-poster bed which had been a family possession for nearly one hundred years. I placed by her bed a little book which I guarded and treasured. It was entitled *The Long Lost Letters of Jenny Lind*. I hope the reader will recall that Jenny Lind had been acclaimed to be the greatest coloratura soprano in her time, 1820-87. She was known as "the Swedish nightingale." In 1850, under the management of P.T. Barnum, she toured the United States. I hoped Roberta would enjoy reading a letter or two and find them intriguing. However, my biggest hope was that she would have a beneficial sleep in her unfamiliar surroundings. The next morning she reported an excellent night.

The following remarks are from the program that night:

> Roberta Peters illuminates the opera and concert stage as one of the pre-eminent artists of the century.
>
> Audiences in the major opera houses of the world, including the standing-room-only crowds which annually throng to her return engagements at The Metropolitan Opera, continue to greet each of her performances with that special adulation reserved for only the brightest stars. She continually reaffirms her consummate command of the concert stage in tours throughout North America and abroad, especially in the Soviet Union, where she became the first native American to win the prestigious Bolshoi Award.
>
> A gracious actress and a singer of incandescent vocal radiance, Roberta Peters is the unmistakable virtuoso of the singing stage.

After the concert, Fred Fox, executive manager of the Arkansas Symphony Orchestra, told me how, before leaving Little Rock that morning, Roberta had requested a copy of the crossword puzzle from the Sunday *New York Times* paper. He did not have the paper, but, since it was early Sunday morning, he quietly rode around the corner and "shop lifted" one from the yard of his good friend and neighbor.

I have not heard about Roberta Peters in the last few years. Yesterday (June 21, 1996), I called her home in Scarsdale, New York. I did what some people might consider unthinkable, but I wanted her to know and approve of the fact that I was writing about her in The Warfield Story.

Obtaining the telephone number from ICM Artists Management that represents her, I put in the call. After the suspense of four rings (thankfully), someone answered. Roberta did not take calls, but I was allowed to speak with her very affable husband, Mr. Bert Fields. I had remembered meeting him in Memphis when Roberta sang there as guest soloist with the Memphis Symphony Orchestra.

His telephone responses to my questions were warm and friendly. He said Roberta is now in her forty sixth year before the public, taking a limited number of engagements each year.

She is now spending a lot of time in volunteer work which includes being on the Board of the National Endowment for the Arts. She was appointed to this position by President George Bush, and it had to be confirmed by the United States Senate. She also is on the Board of the Metropolitan Opera and the Board of Carnegie Hall.

What a great lady she is and such a splendid useful life Roberta Peters is having. And now, for my last big hope—that one day I may see her again.

The Great American Baritone

September 1980. Sitting on the couch in her living room, Betty Faust and I looked at the Warfield Concerts Schedule for 1980-81. We both agreed that this should be the best season we have ever had.

"There is a considerable variety of high quality performances," I remarked. "Ballet, symphony, musicals, operas, choruses, piano, but best of all, the exciting solo recital by that extremely attractive Sherrill Milnes, our Great American Baritone. How fortunate we are to have completed a contract through Herbert Barrett Management company for January 7, 1981, with the very-much-in-demand opera star of the Metropolitan Opera." The fee was $10,000.

I had greatly enjoyed hearing him sing at the Metropolitan Opera in New York, several times with Opera Memphis, and, of course, numerous occasions on television. I had even watched him conduct a master class in Memphis.

Sherrill Milnes is a tall handsome man with heavy

dark hair, gray blue eyes, and a radiant smile that transmits warm friendliness to everyone. He always smiles except, perhaps, on stage in roles such as Iago or Scarpia or some of the other villainous characters created for baritones and basses.

His accompanist was Jon Spong, who, Sherrill said, had been his good friend ever since their college days. Indeed, they were a contrasting pair, Jon short and Sherrill tall, but when performing together, the beautiful music they produced was magic.

The thought of Sherrill Milnes on the Warfield Concert Series was indeed thrilling. Although it was only September, Betty and I decided we would start immediately with publicity on Mr. Milnes. We rented a marvelous film he had made in Italy at the home of Verdi. I had seen this film at a meeting of AMICI (friends of the Metropolitan) in Mississippi and felt that showing it here would be the best possible way to impress our prospective audience with Sherrill Milnes and his magnificent voice.

All kinds of extra equipment were needed: a projection machine (bulky and hard to manage), a suitable screen, and a dark room, but we did not mind, and we had a good time.

We went to the civic clubs such as Rotary, Kiwanis, Lions, Altrusa, and to several other places such as the library and museum to make a talk and to show the movie. The immediate response was most gratifying. Even those with no musical interest expressed appreciation and pleasure.

I even used the Milnes film at my 71st birthday party by having a black-out room where guests could slip in for a little while to hear some of their favorite Verdi baritone arias. When the party was over, my daughter Libby and I went in the dark room to relax and watch the whole movie again; we were completely enraptured by what we heard.

Things were going well. The month of October had given us cooler weather. The leaves turned to yellow, red, and gold. The stately sweetgum and oak trees were particularly handsome that year. Now in November, a light frost brought a warning to use winter clothes.

We had already presented three successful concerts. The one on November ninth, a pops concert, by the Memphis Symphony Orchestra and guest artists Anita Darian and Gordon McRae, had filled every seat in the house. There was just one little snag in the very beginning of that concert (I can laugh about it now).

The bus carrying the orchestra arrived late. The bus driver evidently became confused. He drove past Lily Peter Hall and on out of town before he or the orchestra realized that they had been in Helena. The error caused a forty-five minute delay in opening the program.

Fortunately, Gordon McRae came in his private car and he "saved the day" by coming out on stage and making jokes and humorous comments until the bus had turned around and arrived with the musicians. Never has a seventy-five member symphony assembled as rapidly and started playing.

More trouble was yet to come. When the program ended and the players were leaving the stage, a freak accident occurred. A cello was knocked off stage into the orchestra pit. The owner of this highly valuable instrument kept his dignity. He walked down the steps, and quietly picked it up. I do not know the extent of the damage, but he said it was well insured.

My exuberance over the January seventh appearance of Sherrill Milnes had reached an all-time high. I planned to have a reception afterward and to have a small dinner party the night before for the two artists. Everything was going to be perfect.

Then BANG! A complication arose and the complication was *me*. I had a heart attack. All those enchanting plans were swept away.

It happened on Sunday, November 17, 1980. After going to church and singing in the choir, I joined my good friend, Mary Burch, for lunch at the Helena Country Club. Winston was not hungry and said to go on without him.

We were happily eating dessert, a generous piece of rich chocolate pie covered with Cool Whip (the days of real whipped cream even then were gone), when a sharp gripping pain shot through my shoulders and chest. It only lasted a few seconds. I said nothing to Mary, finished our meal and started home.

On the way, another stabbing pain charged briefly through my chest. I only experienced one more severe attack, but that was enough to make Winston take me to the emergency room of the Helena Hospital, now known as the Helena Regional Medical Center.

My EKG showed nothing abnormal. The internist in charge was a large, heavy-set woman enveloped in a voluminous green uniform. She moved slowly from one patient to another. "Nothing alarming" she said to me. "Take this tranquilizer and go home for a little rest." In my mind, I felt it would require at least a mild catastrophe to alarm that bundle of green.

In spite of the negative results, we went to Memphis the next morning for me to have a complete physical; I felt confident that the results would be all right. Such was the case until Dr. John Hughes received the electrocardiograph report. Without mincing any words he announced, "You have had a heart attack."

Immediately, a wheelchair arrived. With my hat, coat, purse, and gloves, I was wheeled into Intensive Care. The busy nurse looked utterly puzzled to receive a patient arriving dressed as if for a trip and also feeling surprisingly well.

I stayed there several days amid those bright lights (they were never turned off), monitors, constant attention, and no chance to sleep. I was not seriously ill, but was told to give up unnecessary activities and rest for the next few months.

That left Helen Benton and Betty Faust, the other two Warfield Committee members, with all the responsibility for the Sherrill Milnes concert, and me exceedingly disappointed and unable to be a part of it.

Helen Benton and her husband, Bill, offered to meet the 6 P.M. plane, which brought Sherrill and Jon to Memphis on January 6th, a cold rainy winter night. She called me from the airport at about seven-thirty to report, "We're still waiting. I'm worried about my rolls. The nice dinner I have for them will be ruined." I tried to console her and said, "The supper will easily keep. Let me know when you are back here."

About ten o'clock the telephone rang, "All is well. We have finished eating. Come on over for a little visit."

I turned to Winston. "Hurry! At last we are going to talk with Sherrill Milnes."

Every inch of the Benton's palatial home is attractive. The earthy colors and soft lights in the spacious family room must have been a soothing ambience for the tired travelers. There they were—a picture of homelike contentment, Helen, Bill and the two artists sat in front of a roaring fire after eating wild duck, rice and gravy, hot rolls, vegetables, and a dessert of sumptuous pecan pie—a night to remember.

Twenty-four hours later, the 1,200-seat Lily Peter Auditorium was ablaze with lights, the bustling crowd rushing in impatient to find suitable seats. After all, using a free ticket to hear a whole evening of Sherrill

Milnes was a momentous occasion.

Continuing to limit activities because of my recent heart attack, I could not join the throng, but was allowed to sit in a comfortable chair in a wing of the stage with a blanket for drafts. Actually, I felt advantageously seated and was fascinated to hear Sherrill vocalizing nearby.

Soon he paused for a few minutes and walked over to speak to me. In his hand was one of the coveted Milnes buttons. Three inches in diameter it showed the smiling face of Mr. Milnes and across the top the words, "Milnes is Magnificent." This he bestowed on my shoulder. Surprised and honored, I thanked him profusely. I also told him how much I enjoyed his vocal warm-up exercises.

The committee wanted some kind of little act of recognition for Sherrill, but what we knew not. Presenting a lavish bouquet of flowers to a man was not exactly appropriate. Every idea seemed unsuitable, and what we finally did, as I now think back, turned out not nearly as well as expected. At best, it added a touch of humor to the performance.

We arranged to give Mr. Milnes a fair-size key to the city amply decorated with ribbon streamers and a couple of small flowers. The reigning Miss Helena was engaged to make the presentation and instructed do it the minute he finished his last song.

She arrived at the auditorium dressed in her pageant ball gown and crown, "pretty as a picture" we used to say, and inconspicuously sat in a far side of the orchestra pit ready to go on stage with our gift at the proper moment.

Enjoying every note, I was blissfully tucked under my blanket in the stage wing as the beautiful recital proceeded.

Near the end of the program, our artist sang Charles Gounod's "Avant de quitter ces lieux" from the opera, *Faust*. In the middle of the aria, he paused for a couple of seconds. Suddenly I saw Miss Helena grandly coming toward Sherrill with the key. Oh, *no*! I could not believe my eyes because I knew he had paused only to take a deep breath and one short side-step. She thought the concert was over. Nevertheless, he smiled graciously accepting the key to the city. Then motioning to the accompanist he finished the aria apparently undisturbed. Our humble apologies followed and were agreeably acknowledged. No more was ever said.

After the recital, Helen Benton entertained with an elaborate reception at her home honoring Sherrill and Jon. It was an elegant affair, and I am sure Sherrill and Jon were impressed with the friendliness of southern hospitality.

They were taken to the airport the next day by Nina Hornor, who for a long time was one of our most dependable and capable ushers. A tall stately lady in her middle years, whom nature has favored with beauty, she always dressed, when on duty, in a long evening gown. She knew everybody and had the ability to put people at ease, but she also kept an eagle eye on the audience, ready for any disturbance or problem which might occur. Nina returned from the airport trip the recipient of a "Milnes is Magnificent" button.

Four Years Later

Sherrill Milnes, our great American baritone, returned to Helena for a second solo recital on Friday, March 8, 1985, almost exactly two months from the date of his fiftieth birthday, January 10, 1985 (according to Musical America Magazine). Again, Jon Spong was his accompanist.

This time, being fully recovered from any heart problems, I took part in everything.

His performance price had increased. Our contract read $22,000. To this day, that amount remains the highest sum the Warfield Committee has ever paid for a concert. Our dear generous Miss Lily gave us a contribution of $10,000 toward the bill, and that was the only reason we could afford it.

In contrast to Mr. Milnes' previous visit, he arrived in the afternoon; the day was sunny and unusually warm. Katherine Hill and I were waiting at the gate.

I remember Sherrill's remark when we walked out of the airport: "Feel the good warm air." Since out-of-doors temperatures affected vocal chords, his two delicate strings should have been pleased with such desirable atmosphere.

He chose the front seat with Katherine, leaving the back to Jon and me for our ride to Helena, a golden opportunity to talk with Jon, the highly regarded organist and vocal coach who might give me advice about our choir at St. John's. At the present time of this writing, I have sung in the choir there for the last sixty-eight years and often served as substitute choir director, finally directing for a continual period of twenty years.

We discussed choral music. I discovered that he too liked Charles Gaunod's "Sanctus" from the "St. Cecilia" Mass. We agreed it was one of the most heavenly pieces of sacred music. The Sanctus will always be my favorite.

In the front, Katherine and Sherrill were absorbed in talking about the pros and cons of farming methods in the Delta. The expansive acres of farmland we passed along the way were a contrast to his early life on the farm in Downers Grove, Illinois.

Soon the bridge came into view, and then the Holiday Inn where they were left with instructions that Katherine would call for them at seven for dinner at my house. The only other people expected were Nina Hornor and her husband Elmer.

Two previous experiences with singers had sent me home to cook beefsteak for them in the middle of the afternoon preceding an evening performance. Thus, I felt comparatively safe in selecting a beef roast for Mr. Milnes. The *piece de resistance* on the menu was a homemade blackberry cobbler; he flattered me by asking for seconds on both items.

Nina led the conversation with a lively discussion—and a very expedient one on musical instruments. Mr. Milnes could cleverly demonstrate their tones with onomatopoeic sounds. So well did he imitate the French horn that I accused him of playing it without the horn. At that—his startled look was a sign to change the subject.

The concert the following night can be called magnificent, a huge success in every way. Afterward, a reception at my house, and the next morning Sherrill Milnes and Jon Spong returned to New York.

Recently, last February 23, 1996, I attended an Opera Concert in Memphis celebrating the Fortieth Anniversary of Opera Memphis. Sherrill Milnes was one of the seven favorite artists invited to participate in the sensational program.

I had made up my mind to go backstage and speak to him when the concert ended. Of course he would not recognize me—it had been over ten years, the gray hair was now white and my face a mask of wrinkles, but even so it would be exciting.

When the last number, *Sextet* from the opera, *Lucia de Lammermoor*, came to an end and the six opera stars left the stage, I was right behind, and I found Mr. Milnes still standing in the wing and introduced myself. He smiled pleasantly, and in a few seconds said, "How is that piano?" In complete surprise, I knew then that he was referring to the time he scratched his name on my piano with an icepick. How nice that he remembered.

Raining Roses

Not only were opera stars Roberta Peters and Sherrill Milnes on the Warfield Concert Series, but full length operas—sometimes even grand opera—began to appear in the schedules.

During the early days of Warfield Concerts, the committee did not consider opera. We did not have the money, the facilities, and frankly, the inclination. True to the letter, we had several student productions and one *La Boheme* from the Canadian Opera Company, but none of those were of professional quality.

Serious opera we thought was beyond our reach, too expensive, too over powering for the audiences and more importantly, we did not know where to find a superior touring company. Time overcame these obstacles, which gives me the liberty to do a little tall talking about the impressive opera productions that did take place.

During the year 1980, informative material was received announcing a tour by the National Opera Touring Company, a division of the New York City Opera, with Giuseppe Verdi's opera, *La Traviata*, a favorite of opera lovers.

The National Opera Touring Company was developed by Beverly Sills, who had retired from the Metropolitan Opera company where she had been a widely known coloratura soprano to become General Director of New York City Opera. Her purpose was to bring full-length high-class opera to the American people and also to give American singers the chance they deserved.

To us, the Warfield Committee, the very thought of *La Traviata*, a Frank Casaro production from Beverly Sill's New York City Opera in Lily Auditorium was stupendous. Without any hesitation we would do it. That much was settled.

Dear Friends:

As you know, I am now wearing my new hat as director of the New York City Opera. An exciting part of this venture has been the formation this year of The National Opera Touring Company, a project designed to bring opera productions of the highest caliber to all parts of the United States.

Our first venture will be Verdi's *La Traviata* in Frank Corsaro's production, which has been in the City Opera's repertory for many years. The company will feature City Opera artists, with orchestra and chorus.

I look forward to sharing an exciting season with you.

Warmest regards to you all,
Beverly Sills
General Director, New York City Opera

Already, I had visions of Alfredo singing his famous drinking song, "Libiamo, libiame ne lieti calici" and of the well-favored Violetta, fragile in her loveliness, bursting into the dazzling aria "Sempre - libera ...."

More sobering and realistic thoughts quickly returned as we began to think of finances and a way to take care of all probable expenses.

Following a series of telephone conversations, an agreement was reached on a contract for *La Traviata* fully staged with orchestra on Monday, May 4, 1981, with a reduced price ("strictly confidential" it read) of $18,000. Again Miss Lily promised financial assistance. With arrangements completed much more easily than anticipated, we could begin plans to make our first big-time opera a success.

The National Opera's tour started in New Orleans, then to Meridian, Mississippi, and then on to Helena.

The large truck carrying heavy stage sets, costumes, and lighting equipment arrived at six on the morning of May 4th ready to unload. In spite of the early hour Paula Hickey, our dependable director of the auditorium, and the local men and boys who had been hired as stage hands to help with unloading, were waiting to begin.

A Warfield Concert always gave Paula a busy and troublesome day. She received frequent questions and often important requests, and somehow she could satisfy them. For example keeping an even temperature in the hall was almost impossible. Ballet dancers wanted the stage well heated to stretch their muscles. Conductors and instrumentalists liked to be cold. It was either too hot or too cold and audiences did not hesitate to express their feelings. I, myself, am guilty of being chilly most of the time on the second row while my friends in the rear were fanning. We kept Paula and her key chain running back and forth cutting on and cutting off the system, but she remained calm and tried with much effort to please.

In favor of the workers the weather was warm and clear, the month of May at its best. An accommodating sun shone brightly in a cloudless sky as if to give the visitors a cheery welcome. John Milton so tastefully describes my thoughts:

> *Hail bounteous May, that dost inspire*
> *Mirth, youth and warm desire*
> *Woods and groves are of thy dressing*
> *Hill and dale dost boost thy blessing*

The bus with the cast of thirty-three and thirty eight members of the orchestra drove into town about noon. They were jubilant over the facilities, the large stage, ample dressing rooms, and sharp acoustics. A few confessed that accommodations in New Orleans had not been comfortable, and in Meridian the reception had been lukewarm. No need to worry about Helena. Our plans included throwing roses at the singers and a champagne breakfast after the opera.

In early May the local flower gardens are full of roses more than any other time of year. Bushes are prolific with varieties of gorgeous blossoms. The committee had been invited to cut as many roses as we wanted to use the night of the opera.

Arriving an hour ahead of time at the auditorium, I brought two immense baskets of colorful roses which I put out of sight in the orchestra pit. They had been carefully packed with damp paper towels to maintain freshness.

As the people assembled I asked those sitting on the front row to gather bunches of the roses at intermission in readiness to toss them to the cast during their bows after the final act. We were now set up. With a sigh of relief, I sat down to enjoy the opera.

The orchestra, part of the regular New York City Opera Orchestra, wearing tails and white ties filed into the pit. After they were seated and tuned up by the concert master, the lights dimmed and a spotlight flashed on conductor Brian Salesky who stepped up on the podium, bowed, turned to his musicians and started the overture. I am quite fond of overtures because they introduce bits of the most melodious music in the score.

The performance ran smoothly and professionally. The pleasing voices of the young singers were in full bloom and delightful. Pretty Karen Hunt sang the role of Violetta. She was perfect for the part. Sometime

later, I read in *Opera News* of her well-received per-
formance at Kennedy Center in Washington, D.C.
Karen returned to Helena in October, 1985, singing the
role of Marguerite in Gounod's *Faust* with the Kansas
City Lyric Opera when it was included in the Warfield
Series Schedule for that year. She highlighted that per-
formance with her rendition of Marguerite's "Jewel
Song."

Tenor Tonio Di Paolo sang opposite her as Alfredo.
His voice projected well, and he gave a credible interpretation of the amorous Alfredo. Since then, Tonio
has had principal parts in numerous regional operas.

I continued to worry for fear our roses would not
stay fresh, but they did. When the last act was almost
over and Violetta was sadly dying of tuberculosis, I
tapped the shoulders of those in front of me to alert
them that in a few minutes we would do our own little
act.

Violetta gasped her last breath, and Alfredo lay
stricken with grief. Then the curtain was pulled together. When in a few seconds it opened again and the
bows started in front of standing ovations and thun-
derous applause, roses rained on the stage. What fun
we had! What a thrilling surprise for the cast. They
beamed with pleasure and Violetta threw kisses to the
crowd. Without a doubt our first big-time opera was a
triumphant success. So was the champagne breakfast
that followed immediately at Habib's on Main Street
in Helena.

June 18, 1981
Ms. Helen C. Mosby Chairman,
Warfield Concerts P.O. Box 127
Helena, Arkansas 72342

Dear Ms. Mosby:

Thank you for your letter, which I received when I returned last week from a month in China. I am so glad you enjoyed the performance of our National Opera Touring Company, and I do appreciate your having taken the time to write.

With kindest regards.

Sincerely,
Beverly Sills
General Director

Again, roses were used to decorate the various individual tables covered with white linen cloths and napkins. At one table there were several Memphis visitors including Mrs. Ethel Maxwell, a well-known voice teacher and coach, and one of her students, bass soloist Charles Billings. But the star of the party was opera conductor Brian Salesky. He played familiar tunes on the piano and then walked among the tables laughing and talking with the guests. Brian seemed to know exactly the right thing to say to make a person feel important.

Although the champagne breakfast honored the principals of *La Traviata*, we did not forget the rest of the cast. They were entertained with a supper party in the dining hall of the Fine Arts Center.

Seven times New York City National Opera came to Helena as a Warfield Concert. Following *La Traviata* we had Bizet's *Carmen* on January 15, 1983, with Adria Firestone, a flashy bewitching Carmen, and Robert McFarland, a swaggering Escamillo the toreador. McFarland returned here in the title role of Verdi's *Rigoletto* on March 23, 1985 with Joyce Guyer as Gilda and tenor Michael Sylvester as the Duke of Mantua. Michael is now enjoying a major career at the Metropolitan Opera.

Robert McFarland was a most welcome guest in my home during the two days City Opera stayed in town for *Rigoletto*. The morning after the performance (Sunday), he delighted me as well as the congregation of St. John's Episcopal Church by singing a solo for the offertory. A rare treat it was.

New York City Opera National Company brought us a beautifully staged production of Puccini's *Madame Butterfly* on April 3, 1987. The opening scene, showing in realistic flavor a tranquil Japanese garden, was greeted with expressions of pleasure by the audience.

February 23, 1988, was the date for the *Barber of Seville* (*Il Barbiere di Siviglia* by Gioachino Rossini), a lively comic opera easy to watch and not too long. As much as I love opera, I will have to admit that some of them are quite lengthy and would be more enjoyable if shortened slightly.

A second *La Traviata*, again by the National Opera Touring Company, came here on March 9, 1989, though with different sets and of course a different cast. Sandra Ruggles as Violetta and Robert Brubaker as Alfredo were outstanding in their parts. The excellent blend of voices in duets and choral groups deserves much praise.

We did have, however, a painful experience in the behavior of the sullen technical crew, who said they hated everything below the Mason-Dixon line. Surprisingly, because every other opera production had run smoothly, the locals and professionals worked agreeably together. Perhaps they were tired from a long tour, but their insulting language and crude remarks were unacceptable.

In addition, this unaccommodating group of technicals refused to draw the curtain (a handsome new onc only a year old) between acts even though we had a man standing by to do it. The whole opera was performed with the stage wide open. At intermission, the crowd was amused by watching the sets being changed, particularly interesting when Violetta's bed was put up and fell down four consecutive times.

Slow to move the loading up after the conclusion of the last scene caused Maureen, our coordinator, to remain at the auditorium until 3 A.M.

Bad news travels fast, and both Columbia Artists Management and Headquarters of the opera were made aware of the unfortunate episode. We soon received sincerely apologetic letters which were wholeheartedly accepted. We have always been good friends with New York City Opera and want to remain so.

To prove our true faith, we contracted the National Opera Touring Company for Mozart's *The Marriage of Figaro* (*La Nozze di Figaro*), a sequel to the *Barber of Seville* for March 8, 1991, another comic opera certain to please one and all.

Besides the New York City Opera, three other companies sent us excellent productions.

On Sunday, October 20, 1985, the well established Kansas City Lyric Opera Company brought Gounod's tragic opera *Faust* to the Twin Cities (Helena-West Helena). *Faust* is an opera of tremendous dramatic appeal that touches all emotions, a splendid performance.

The part of Faust was played by Gran Wilson, an exceptionally talented bel canto tenor. Michael Riley as Mephistopheles and Karen Hunt (her second time here) as the young Marguerite added more impressive singing to the production. We were honored to have Russell Patterson as music director and conductor. Mr. Patterson was also chief conductor of the Kansas City Symphony Orchestra.

Texas Opera Theater, the touring branch of the Houston Grand Opera, brought another tragic opera to Lily Peter Auditorium on March 17, 1990, *Romeo and Juliette*, also by Charles Gounod. I am familiar with

Gounod's works of sacred music as well as opera, and to me, every note he ever wrote was beautiful. Although *Romeo and Juliette* has been considered musically inferior to *Faust*, it has maintained its place in public favor since the day of its premiere.

Shakespeare gave us two popular characters in his *Romeo and Juliet*. Many young people today recognize those names. Some I have known like to think of themselves as either Romeos or Juliets.

Opera Nationale Italiano and The Staat Opera Budapest Orchestra under Stefano Pellegrino performed *Rigoletto* at Lily Peter Auditorium on October 19, 1992. How lucky we were to be able to have a genuine Italian opera on that S.D. Warfield stage, and it was FREE.

I can imagine S.D. now, immaculately dressed in his tuxedo, applauding this spectacular performance in ecstasy over every musical phrase. He would have loved it, but I may have been his good substitute because my own pleasure reached a pinnacle of enjoyment that might very well have paralleled his.

Dressed in a long evening gown for this elegant occasion, I sat in my usual seat on the end of the second row and absorbed every moment of the grandeur of the evening.

It was through Bill Weir, experienced in artist management companies but then working alone, that we negotiated a contract of $18,000 for *Rigoletto*, a bargain if there ever was one. Bill expertly put together the opera company and worked out an extensive tour. Helena was in the direction of the tour. They had an extra unscheduled night and needed a stop. Therefore, we could have *Rigoletto* at what Bill Weir called a "give-away price."

We have not had an opera here since then. I keep hoping the present Warfield Committee can manage to bring one again soon. I know they are trying.

Mr. Opera

For a long time I have listened as often as possible to the Saturday afternoon Nationwide radio broadcasts (sponsored by Texaco) of the Metropolitan Opera in New York City. The intermission features, "Opera News on the Air," I have enjoyed as much or even more than the opera.

Saturday afternoon during the opera season became a special time for me. I allowed myself the anticipated privilege of using our big lounge chair by the radio, a suitable spot to wholly relax and absorb all that could be heard. With a cup of tea or a cold drink, that was attending the opera in comfort.

These opera afternoons occasionally turned into little parties when a few friends would decide to join me. The most frequent visitor was our benefactor, the late S.D. Warfield. He considered opera the pinnacle of culture and sophistication. He would arrive expecting the music to create for him a state of ethereal beauty far removed from the concerns of daily living. A touching aria or a brilliant orchestral passage could cause his emotions to overflow. Forgetting himself, he would arise waving his arms as if conducting the performance. Nothing pleased him more than to be teasingly called Maestro Warfield. Truthfully, his ebullience gave us a lift—albeit it was slightly extreme. We did enjoy ourselves.

It was back in 1946, when millions of listeners first heard the cheerful voice saying, "Good Afternoon Ladies and Gentlemen." For years, after cordially greeting his radio audience, the voice continued to give a thoroughly understandable musical and dramatic analysis of certain aspects of the opera and illustrated his points on the piano.

These intermission talks gave me a deeper appreciation of the art and an interest which served me well through the years. The voice we heard was that of the illustrious Boris Goldovsky who, because of his popular broadcasts, acquired the unofficial title of Mr. Opera.

What he said was not a synopsis but rather his own unique ideas about the music and the libretto. He could even be quite humorous and clever, as was the case with *The Rise and Fall of the City of Mahagonny* by Kurt Weill.

I am familiar with this opera, having seen it in Memphis when the Metropolitan Opera was still touring. I disliked what I saw and heard to the point of almost feeling ill. Being partial to traditional Italian and French Opera, I could not see how the Metropolitan would include such an unappealing performance on their tour. My reaction was shared by others who sat nearby. There seemed to be no favorable comments, but after a day or two, I was absorbed in other things and thought no more about the disappointing opera.

Time moved on, and then one day I had the opportunity to read some of the scripts from Mr. Goldovsky's "Good Afternoon Ladies and Gentlemen" broadcasts. Unexpectedly, my eye came upon the script of *The Rise and Fall of the City of Mahagonny* (broadcast December 22, 1979). I began to read, and noticed immediately great humor.

He began by explaining the pronunciation of the word, *Mahagonny*: not *Ma Hog' a ny* like the name for the wood used for fine furniture, nor like *ma ha go' ny*. He said that it was an invented word for the name of an imaginary city in America and was pronounced *Ma-ha gunny*. To quote him directly, "Since I also had some difficulty getting used to this pronunciation, I trained myself by saying, 'Mahagunny is a place of milk and honey to which the main character comes with lots of money and at the end is sentenced to the electric chair because of lack of munney.'"

I learned from the Goldovsky script that German artists in the nineteen twenties were fascinated with the United States and the tales about gangsters, prohibition, speakeasies, and the electric chair. Such lurid stories must have inspired composer Kurt Weill and librettist Bertolt Brecht to do their opera about

America. Boris Goldovsky's script has made me feel much more kindly about *Mahagonny*. I might even like to see it again.

This great man was born in Russia in 1908. He began his life in music as a child performer on the piano. He and his mother, a prominent concert violinist, fled Russia after the Revolution to live in Berlin, where Boris studied piano under Arthur Schnabel (Schnabel pianos bear his name), and where his mother concertized.

The nineteen thirties brought both Goldvoskys to America and to the Curtis Institute in Philadelphia. Multi-talented Boris gained national recognition. There he studied, taught, conducted, and started his astonishing career in the staging of opera, which was enhanced by his charm, wittiness, and sense of humor.

Boris Goldovsky came to Helena to do a program (November 7, 1988) on the Warfield Series, called *Opera Highlights*. The committee decided to dedicate the concert to Frances Greer, Helena's own former Metropolitan Opera singer. Mrs. Greer is now retired and lives with her husband, Jack Riley, in Ann Arbor, Michigan.

I can remember hearing her sing "Mighty Lak a Rose" on a school program when she was about age five. She amazed friends with the strength and fine quality of her voice which developed as she grew into an exceedingly beautiful lyric soprano. After graduating from Louisiana State University, majoring in voice, Frances was encouraged and coached by her first teacher, Nina Beisel, to enter the Metropolitan Auditions of the Air—a contest sponsored by Sherwin Williams Paint Company—and won first place. In 1940, she received a contract with the Metropolitan Opera. One of her greatest triumphs took place in Memphis at the MOAT (Memphis Open Air Theater) where she sang operetta for several summers. Her thrilling obligato in *Naughty Marietta* aroused such tremendous ovations from the audience that she encored it eight consecutive times.

A letter from Frances Greer after being told that Opera Highlights was dedicated to her reads as follows:

> *11/2/88 Dear Helen: In a few days the concert takes place and Helena will enjoy the great privilege of seeing and hearing a very great artist. Perhaps I told you the two regrets of my life are not having worked with Maestro Goldovsky and Toscanini. I doubt if he knows me at all but please greet him warmly for me. I will be there in spirit and thank you. Love, Frances.*

The three singers with *Opera Highlights* were Candace Goetz, Caroline Thomas, and Michael Willson—all three most attractive with eminently good voices. Their arias, duets, and trios were well received.

The two girls stayed at the home of Betty Faust, and Boris and Michael were my house guests. I honored them with a supper party the night before the concert.

At the party we asked Boris to "play something for us on the piano." He agreed to perform, but not until he had tested the piano for defects. Thankfully, my Baldwin grand had been tuned and sounded extra well for those experienced hands of one of the greatest musicians of our time. He played a piece by Chopin, drawing lively applause from the party guests.

I enjoyed our musical conversations while they were here, but we talked about mathematics too, specifically, a formula which Mr. Goldovsky had worked out how to square instantly any two digit number with 5 as the second of the two digits. As an example:

Take the next highest number of the first number of the two digits. Multiply them. Then add 25. It always works. As an example: 65 x 65, multiply 6 x 7 = 42. Add 25. The answer immediately is 4225. Another example, 85 x 85. Multiply 8 x 9 = 72. Add 25. Immediately the answer is 7225.

Since music demands some math, such as the counting of time within the measures, it is not surprising that Boris could juggle figures.

With his permission in writing, I give you his quotation about opera which can be found on the back cover of his biography, *My Road to Opera*: "Skeptics take heart. I began my road to opera not only in ignorance but with hostility. I have come to embrace this special world with a deep and profound love; and it has been my honor to discover matchless musical talents. Such a reward for a convert!"

To Boris Goldovsky, music is his friend and his religion. He has been known to say that "wherever I am on the podium or at the keyboard, I am very close to heaven."

Fidus Achates

Duane, whose friendship I both value and appreciate, is the Reverend Duane T. Saba, Rector of St. John's Episcopal Church in Helena, Arkansas.

He arrived here January 1, 1975, at the optimistic age of thirty two, a gentle man with a kind heart. Of middle stature, he has black hair and dark eyes that quickly reflect understanding, joy, or sympathy. For members of his church as well as for other friends, be they blessedly young or unquestionably old, he is always there in time of need. He abundantly gives of himself to whatever may be the cause.

As I think back over more than eight eventful decades including two world wars, the stock market crash of 1929, and the great depression of the early thirties, thirty-two seems refreshingly young. Nevertheless, Duane assumed the ministerial duties of this old historic parish filled with tradition.

The first services of the Episcopal Church in Arkansas were held in a private home in Helena in 1839 by the Right Reverend Leonidas Polk who served as a missionary bishop in the Episcopal

Church. I would like to add that he was a graduate of West Point Military Academy but fought in the Confederate Army in the War Between the States and was killed in action. He has been remembered as the fighting bishop.

Considered one of the most beautiful churches in Arkansas, the present St. John's Church building of dark red brick includes a tower and bell and comfortably seats over five-hundred people. It is a combination of Norman and Gothic styles of architecture often called Old English. The interior of the church is cruciform, the east and west transepts forming the arms of a Latin cross that is completed by the main body of the church. The ceilings are vaulted, and enormous globular lighting fixtures trimmed in wrought iron hung from them. The fixtures are supported by weighty black iron chains, giving a sense of vastness.

Enhancing the interior are ecclesiastical furnishings and decorative fixtures of the highest quality. There are massive columns on each side where steps lead up to the chancel. The communion rail, the altar, pulpit, and the lectern are heavily ornamented with lettering, crosses, and designs of wheat and grapes—all made of solid brass.

But the breath-taking beauty within lies in the rich warm glow of the stunning stained glass windows. Their radiant colors depict scenes from the scriptures and include a tall figure of Jesus over the altar, which gleams on a sunny day with a spiritual flow that touches the soul.

The most famous of all these magnificent windows is found in the Narthex, constructed and signed by Tiffany Decorating Company of New York. It is a hallowed spot that fascinates eager tourists.

Sitting in my little place through years in the choir stalls, I continue to be filled with awe and thankfulness for the opportunity to worship the Lord in our noble building, and I shake my head in amazement over the accomplishments of our forefathers. To attempt such a structure today would require a miracle. I hope our young people and new-comers may experience some of my awesome thankfulness when they attend services.

Duane Saba faced tradition from every source. The parishioners, particularly the older ones who, of course, were the financial backbone of the church, were "set in their ways." They did not want to change. They wanted the 1928 prayer book and the old hymnal. To their horror some of the favorite hymns (as an example "Jesus Calls Us o'er the Tumult" or "What A Friend We Have In Jesus") were not even printed in the new hymnals. They wanted to sit in the same well-used pews occupied by beloved ancestors and pray the same prayers their grandparents had prayed.

To do away with old prayer books and hymnals were the orders that came, and Duane courageously started to work on the formidable task of changing St. John's services. I know he must have suffered unlimited discouragement.

He moved slowly and pleasantly, and the Reverend Duane Saba won! Today St. John's has changed (we even have a splendid new organ), and Duane has the admiration of the entire congregation.

I have enjoyed watching him grow and develop into a prominent citizen in the community with his wife Madge, a registered nurse teaching at Phillips County College of the University of Arkansas, and their two children. Corey is working toward her Masters Degree in Memphis, and Michael is a sophomore at the University of Arkansas.

Duane is one of the three appointers for the Warfield Concerts Committee. That means that as Rector of the Episcopal Church, he has the authority of appointing one person of the three concert committee members. I have asked him to write a few remarks about the Warfield Concerts and what they meant to him.

According to Duane:

When I became Rector of St. John's Episcopal Church I also acquired another serious responsibility which created a most enjoyable and interesting dimension to my life.

Having the authority to appoint one of the three Warfield Committee members has made me appreciate the tremendous work they do in presenting concerts to please a public of many varied tastes in music.

For me the cultural element I have received is important, something I have not experienced since my youthful trumpet-playing days when I was growing up in Bismarck, North Dakota. Twice Warfield artists have sung solos in our church following a Saturday night performance. Lyric soprano Shegemi Matsumoto on Sunday, March 2, 1976, thrilled the congregation with Mozart's "Alleluia." Then, to show how American she had become, did a verse of the "Battle Hymn of the Republic."

The other artist was baritone Robert McFarland on March 24, 1985. The night before he had sung the title role in *Rigoletto* with the New York City National Opera Company but Sunday morning he appeared rested and said, "I am pleased to sing here. My busy career has not allowed me to attend church regularly and I am grateful for this unexpected opportunity to use my voice in such a beautiful church."

Because of Warfield Concerts, the music at St. John's on Mother's Day, May 13, 1984, was made charmingly special. Brigham Young University Ambassadors on their Spring tour that year spent the week-end in Helena giving a Warfield Concert on Saturday night, May 12, at Lily Peter Auditorium.

At the request of Helen Mosby, they came to our church the next morning and sang two appropriate pieces for the offertory music. The graciousness of those friendly young students and the refreshing quality of their voices was a treat I shall always remember. The group did not request any payment, but the ladies of the church gave them a light lunch in the undercroft afterward.

Every year I look forward to reading the new concert schedule when it is announced in September and to think that all of it is FREE. Amazing! Even more amazing is the thought that Warfield Concerts will continue into perpetuity.

At the time of this writing (December 4, 1996) Duane is courageously coping with cancer. Through chemotherapy and radiation treatments he continues to hold services, preach on Sunday, and attend to other church duties. His steadfast strength amazes the parishioners who are confident he will recover as Duane smiles with optimism.

The following article appeared in a recent issue of our church paper, *The Evangelist*:

From the Rector: Why Me? Why *Not* Me?

As I begin writing this article on Monday morning, I face returning to Memphis this afternoon to consult with my doctor about a newly discovered tumor in my colon. This was discovered in an examination last Thursday, November 7. The doctor was certain it was cancer; however, he also seems to think it has no connection with the malignant breast tumor that was removed a couple of months ago.

One of the common questions that comes with cancer is "why me? But another more important question is why not me?" Everyone in the world has to battle with evil ... all the time, and usually we each have at least one large dramatic encounter with evil ... a major confrontation sometime in our lives.

It seems there are two kinds of evil. One is human

evil—or evil caused by human beings' misuse of their own free will. In my life I have had to put up with amazingly little of this kind of evil. I have generally gotten along with people and they have gotten along with me. I missed having to go to any of our wars. I have been surrounded by a lot of loving people. So human evil I haven't had to battle as much as most people.

The second kind of evil is natural evil. Human beings don't cause this evil as far as we know. It is evil in nature itself. Earthquakes, tornadoes, or human disease such as polio, Alzheimer's disease, arthritis, heart disease and cancer are among this second kind of evil.

I have had very little experience with this kind of evil in my life, although I have been given a great amount of preparation for battle with it. Look at the preparation God has given me:

I have had 53 years of almost perfect health.

I have been paid by my job to study this evil and to be intellectually fortified to battle with it.

Again, my job has enabled me to explore the spiritual resources to deepen my own personal relation with God, which is the greatest armor against natural evil, too!

And God has placed me in the context of loving Christian communities. First my own family, and second my bigger family, this Church, both of which have provided intense love and caring support.

With all that preparation and help I am certainly better qualified than most people to take on a serious battle with natural evil. Why not me? It doesn't seem unjust at all. Remember for all of us, fighting, resolving, defeating evil (of one form or the other) is a major part of life.

For Jesus, the essence of His life was seen on the cross where He took on Himself the worst of human evil. In Jesus, God joined us in the battle with evil. God is always joining us in this effort.

The battles with evil can be known as Good, because they can be occasions of love—That's when we can know more than ever God's presence and support. He has been doing that for me through the Christian community—through you.

Well, I have needed you and you have been there, and I will continue to need you and I am sure you will continue to let God use you in supporting me in this battle with natural evil. In fact, your love and prayers have been so powerful that I couldn't feel more ready for the operation that I will face in the next few weeks. I feel like one of those circus performers that get shot out of a cannon. I feel like I am being shot out of your cannon of love and prayer aimed at Memphis. I couldn't be more supported. I thank you, and I thank God for being with us. Amen.

The Seed

Rosalind deserves the credit, or even more, the honor, for having the first thought ever given to the idea of a music festival.

Rosalind Mundt Solomon, wife of Aubrey Solomon, was a graduate of the Cincinnati Conservatory of Music. She majored in violin performance and was an experienced choral director with perfect pitch and who apparently knew more about classical music than anyone in this area. I respected her knowledge and her opinions if the subject was musical. One of her very own quotations was, "I will compromise on anything but music." She agreed with Samuel Johnson who said, "Music is the only sensual pleasure without vice."

It was a privilege to sing under Rosalind's expert direction. She had the gift of pulling music out of a person if any was there to pull. I often told her, "Rosalind, when I see you standing in front of us with that inspired look on your face I KNOW you expect my best possible effort. I always gave her every ounce of sound I had. In return, my vocal abilities increased, and I acquired a deeper understanding of the dynamics and interpretation used in choral singing.

Being the same age and friends since childhood, she and I worked well together on the initial Warfield Committee. We were overwhelmed with the potential that could be foreseen in the development of these free concerts, and we were dedicated to using the much appreciated yearly income from the Warfield Trust Fund to the greatest advantage.

In the early months of the first year (1968), Rosalind and I were engaged in numerous conversations in which we exchanged ideas about fantastic concerts for the future. We imagined all sorts of spectacular performances. We would certainly have nothing but the best.

One time she casually mentioned, "Some day it would be nice to have a music festival." "Yes, that would be fun," I agreed. No more was said on the subject, but unknowingly she had planted a sturdy little seed in my mind that was to stay silently there for the next 18 years.

Rosalind's health began to fail as she suffered with high blood pressure. After three years of service, she reluctantly resigned from the committee and a few years later died while recovering from a mild stroke.

Her death saddened a host of friends, those in the music world, the members of Temple Beth El, and especially her Beech Street neighbors. They loved her cooking, such mouth-watering delicacies as cakes, pies, cheese straws, or salted pecans that she often-times sent them.

I missed her too. Our friendship had been strangely enriched by the fact that she did not know how to drive an automobile or own one. I drove her to and from the concerts, took her to meetings, and she rode with me to the Memphis airport when it was necessary to meet an artist arriving for a concert. These rides offered time for pleasantly intimate talking and left me with indelible memories.

In the following years, the Warfield Committee presented some of the "spectacular concerts" that Rosalind and I had dreamed of.

April 18, 1975, brought the highly acclaimed Milwaukee Symphony conducted by Kenneth Shermerhorn, with violinist Shlomo Mintz as the guest artist. This was a rare treat for the Warfield audience who appreciated the elegance of a whole evening of classical music. The fee (which seemed enormous) was $8,500 and was partly funded by Miss Lily Peter. Miss Lily was always happy to have a completely classical performance in the auditorium that was named for her. She also felt that her donations would encourage us to aspire to big names and good music in planning our schedules. How many times in later years we were to wish for Miss Lily's help.

Conductor Schermerhorn has had many splendid triumphs since then. He has conducted at the Metropolitan Opera and been guest conductor with other big-time symphonies. Young Shlomo Mintz matured to be recognized as a world-famous solo violinist. I am glad to have heard him in his early years.

After lengthy negotiations and shuffling around dates, the full Atlanta Symphony Orchestra conducted by celebrated Robert Shaw played in Lily Peter Auditorium on March 21, 1984. We could have this prestigious body of musicians because they were unsuccessful in filling that March 21st date in a larger city. Pushed to finish setting up their tour schedule, they agreed to a Helena performance for $18,000.

Twice the New Orleans Philharmonic Symphony Orchestra (October 24, 1979, and February 18, 1982) came to this river town to do a Warfield Concert. Someone in the audience asked me what philharmonic meant. Rather than answer in my own words, I used *Webster's*. Phil comes from the Greek word, *philos*, which means loving. Harmonic is derived from *harmonia*, meaning harmony or loving music. Thus, in a condensed definition, philharmonic means "loving music."

Both occasions gave us superb performances, but the second one had an exceptional flavor. It was presented in memory of Rosalind Solomon. Andrew Massey conducted, and the internationally great cellist Leonard Rose was guest soloist. His cello sang with heartfelt tones during Tchaikovsky's *Variations on a Rococo Theme*; and if there is any communication between heaven and earth, I know Rosalind was happy.

I can remember still the thrill of seeing the big classy Saint Louis Symphony Orchestra (over 100 instruments) assembled on the S.D. Warfield stage, tuning up to begin the concert. A full house expectantly awaited the opening number. This propitious event came about through an acquaintance the committee had with Royce McEuen, area representative for Southwestern Bell Telephone Company, from Forrest City, Arkansas. Royce frequently attended our concerts and realized the importance of them.

The first inkling of this once-in-a-lifetime opportunity was his request to meet with us.

Almost right away the four of us—Betty Faust, Cassie Brothers, Helen Benton, and I sat around Betty's dining room table with Royce to hear what he had to say. A well-dressed gentleman of middle size with graying hair, Royce put everyone at ease with his unaffected cordiality.

He told us that Southwestern Bell Telephone Company and the National Endowment for the Arts, coordinated by Mid-America Arts Alliance, had joined together to sponsor a tour of the Saint Louis Symphony Orchestra. When he said the cost of one performance was $36,000 our eyes nearly popped out of their sockets. Unbelievable! Figures of that proportion we had never thought of.

He quickly continued, "Your part of that total would be $19,000." Even nineteen thousand looked staggering to us, but we looked at each other. Such a chance might not ever come again. No more hesitation, we jubilantly accepted his offer.

Royce soon asked for another meeting. He had in mind some delectable plans. Cassie answered his request by taking us all to the Helena Country Club for lunch, a good place to relax and talk. Royce decided we should have after the concert an elaborate reception in the banquet hall which was across the lobby from the auditorium. Southwestern Bell would bear all expenses for the entire party, and everyone in the audience was to be invited, another windfall for the committee.

All our plans that were successfully executed came to life on April 22, 1988. The concert was perfect, and the reception added a grand finish to this extravagant evening. The hall was bright with lights and vases of flowers. In the center was a gorgeous table of enticing food that could please the taste buds of the most sensitive gourmet. The guests socialized around the table making complimentary comments about the orchestra.

In contrast to America's brilliant symphony orchestras was a stimulating performance by the large symphony orchestra from Prague, Czechoslovakia, on Thursday, October 18, 1982. The contract was $14,000.

The boundary lines of Czechoslovakia have been tossed around by larger more powerful border countries of Poland, Germany, Austria, Hungary, and

Russia. In spite of its political and military turbulence, the Czechs both young and old love music and numbers of their musicians have reached international fame.

The Prague Symphony had an extraordinarily large section of strings who played with remarkable virtuosity throughout the program, which offered selections to please everybody.

After the performance, I entertained the musicians with a reception at my home. It could easily have been called a reception of sign language. The only ones speaking English were the conductor and the manager. However, they liked the food and were able to make known their wishes for vodka. I was glad to accommodate by producing several bottles of vodka, which were very shortly emptied.

The following review from our local paper provides interesting reading:

Prague Symphony draws ovations, bravos, applause

With 90 musicians on stage and an audience filling to capacity the Lily Peter Auditorium, the Warfield Concert last Thursday night by the Prague Symphony Orchestra, directed by Jiri Belohlavek, was an evening of enjoyment long to be remembered. The general opinion of the entire crowd was "a performance which pleased everyone."

An immediate feeling of good will prevailed

between artists and listeners when the program was opened with a beautiful symphonic rendition of the Star Spangled Banner followed by the Czech and Slavic National Anthems.

Most appropriately Bohemian the first number was the bright and fast moving "Bartered Bride Overture" by Smetana. All instruments blended together in rich musical expression showing a well trained ensemble very responsive to its conductor.

A real thrill came when Vladislav Kozderka, trumpet soloist, accompanied by the Prague's exceptionally large and beautiful string section, played Hayden's *Trumpet Concerto* in E flat major. Mr. Kozderka displayed a brilliant virtuosity and stamina of lip and breath control which brought him a standing ovation.

Symphony No. 8 in G major by Dvorak although not as well known as his "New World" was equally as delightful to hear.

—*Helena-West Helena World*
Monday, November 1, 1982.

St. Louis Symphony Orchestra Musicians Committee
May 1, 1988
Helen C. Mosby
Warfield Concerts
P.O. Box 1027
Helena, AR 72342

Dear Ms. Mosby:
On behalf of the musicians of the St. Louis Symphony, we would like to thank you for the lovely reception after our April 22nd Concert. We always appreciate the

opportunity to meet and speak with our audience. The patrons were delightful and the food was both delicious and elegantly displayed. It was an added pleasure to meet so many Arts Council members. Thank you for being such a gracious host. We hope we have the opportunity to enjoy your hospitality again in the future.

With warm regards,
Susan Slaughter, Co-Chairperson
St. Louis Symphony Orchestra Musicians Committee
Morris Jacob, Co-Chairperson
St. Louis Symphony Orchestra Musicians Committee

The 1982-83 Warfield Concerts schedule was one of the best. In addition to the Prague Symphony, there were five other presentations including opera, ballet, a boys choir, the U.S. Concert Band, and a recital. Three of these were from European countries, and all were super-excellent.

Opening this successful season was a recital by violinist Joy Brown Wiener and tenor Raymond Gibbs, both widely acclaimed professional musicians. Memphis born, Mrs. Wiener is presently concertmaster with the Memphis Symphony Orchestra. Since childhood, she has played before large audiences in this country and throughout Europe. At age 15, she was soloist with The Charleston, South Carolina Symphony, The Piedmont Festival Orchestra, and The St. Louis Symphony. She has brought unparalleled distinction to the musical community in this area.

Joy's playing aroused fresh memories among S.D.'s friends who remembered his adulation for her as she started her career and the pleasure he experienced as she developed into a prominent violinist.

When Mr. Gibbs joined the Metropolitan Opera, he was the youngest baritone on the roster. Three years later, he made a triumphant debut as a tenor with the Houston Grand Opera. Since then, he has been heard in leading roles at the Metropolitan Opera and in European Opera Houses. Both he and Joy received abundant applause and many compliments from our audience.

The concert was in memory of Sam Wesley Anderson. Sam was one of the original three Warfield Committee members. He was president and owner of the local KFFA Radio Station and on the board of the Mutual Broadcasting Company. His business experience and service in community affairs were an asset to the Warfield Committee.

His attractive wife, Nita, gladly entertained visiting artists after a concert. Wearing a glamorous party dress, she would graciously greet them. Nita and I laughed over the reception she and Sam had for the popular pianist, Peter Nero, who had filled the auditorium beyond capacity forcing us (with his permission) to put chairs on the stage. She had food aplenty and any kind of drink, but Peter refused all offers with a confession: "I'm an alcoholic and would appreciate a nice big glass of ice water." He was quite pleasant and charmed those who visited with him.

Having served in World War II as an officer in the United States Navy, Sam had kept his commission in the Naval Reserve. His personality reflected patriotism, which inspired us to add a touch of the military to the program.

Arrangements were made for a presentation of the National Colors by the Color Guard of the United States Navy Flying Rifles Drill Team from the not-too-far-away Millington, Tennessee, Naval Air Station to be followed by Raymond Gibbs leading the audience in singing the National Anthem.

This meritorious act was to take place with the artists on stage ready to follow the opening program. Every detail had been taken care of, and we just knew our little scheme would make a crowning hit.

At eight, the lights dimmed, the crowd stopped talking, and we waited. Nothing happened. Where was that COLOR GUARD!? A nervous silence prevailed. Joy Wiener decided to pick up her treasured violin and begin the concert.

Sitting in my usual commanding seat on the end of the second row, I was in despair. I looked back one more time, and to my horror of horrors I saw the Color Guard slowly gliding down the aisle. Joy and violin were in the middle of "Praeludium" from *Partita No. 6* by Bach.

I used to tell the committee that they made me do the "dirty work" meaning the things no one else would do. This time there was no choice. I had to do it! I saw the flags coming closer. As they reached me I simply stretched out my left arm and grabbed the flag bearer's coattails yanking him to a stop. Then in a whisper I said, "Turn around and go back." The startled flag bearer said not a word. He silently turned around, and the disappointed Color Guard glided back up the aisle and out. We did not see them again. What a narrow escape from disaster. I really don't think there was much disturbance.

The beautiful concert proceeded without interruption, and our audience expressed their pleasure with rigorous applause and a standing ovation.

Mrs. Helen Mosby
P.O. Box 127
Helena, AR 72342

Dear Mrs. Mosby:

As requested by your letter of 16 August 1982, a color guard from the Naval Air Technical Training Center has been scheduled to present the National Colors at your special concert on Thursday, 23 September 1982.

Chief Petty Officer H.R. Littlefield and the color guard will arrive in Helena at approximately 5:30 P.M. on the day of the concert.

If you have any further questions or should the concert be canceled, please contact Chief Littlefield.

Sincerely,
M.S. Schrupp
Lieutenant Commander, USN
By direction of the Commanding Officer

An interesting aspect of the concerts from foreign countries has been the impression the performers have of America. The freedom to walk up and down the streets stopping in shops, the abundance of food in the supermarkets, and the friendliness of the people have made them genuinely appreciate the United States.

One of the most talented groups we have ever had, The Grand Ballet from Zagreb, Yugoslavia, performing here on November 10, 1982, experienced some of these feelings which are described in the following article from the *Daily World*:

ZAGREB BALLET MEMBERS ENJOY VISIT, PERFORMANCE IN HELENA

Yugoslavian performers in the Zagreb Ballet have found America beautiful.

What they have seen of the country has mainly been through the window of the bus they are traveling in. The troupe's schedule is so hectic they seldom have time to view the sights of America.

One performer remarked they had to snap pictures through the windows as . they came across the Mississippi River. The group is on a six week tour of America which includes 36 performances.

Tuesday they were in Little Rock, Wednesday in

Helena and Thursday they will perform in Tupelo, Mississippi. Crepinko Andret said, "Your country is beautiful. New Orleans was beautiful. I've never seen that part of the country ... only in a movie." The group began the tour in New York. They went up into Canada and then started south. They are presently working their way back to New York.

The performers are enthusiastic about their shows. "The audience is always full. The public always seems satisfied," Andret said.

Several of the performers said the only problems they were having was the difference in foods and a slight language barrier.

One performer mentioned they were enjoying the weather here. "It is comfortable here. At home it will be cold." The main complaint of the performers was they did not have enough time to see America the way they would like to. "There is not enough time to see. (We) don't have every chance to see America like this. People are very kind. We have a hard time to hear the language," Andret said.

Andret also said there was really no difference in the people from his native country and Americans, "People are people everywhere," he said.

Milena Leben said she has been in America before, but still enjoys the United States very much. She said this was a difficult tour. Despite seven hour practices in Yugoslavia to prepare, the traveling and performing on a new stage every night is hard.

"Everything is going very good. We like very much and always feel the applause. Your country is very different from Europe. Everything is bigger. The food is also different," she said.

The Zagreb Grand Ballet is a major wing of the Croatian National Theatre. It is one of Europe's oldest and highly respected ballet companies. Our audience was fully impressed with the brilliance of their performance, dazzled by the daring leaps and pirouetting of the dancers. For this we paid $7,500—a reduced amount from their usual performance fee.

With immense pressure for free tickets and out-of-towners expected from every direction, the incomparable Vienna Choir Boys reached Helena in a hubub of excitement.

Some of this was curiosity. How would they be dressed? What would they like to eat or could they speak English? From the advanced publicity material we received, their lives were disciplined and organized.

Some indication of the regard in which they were held may be gleaned from a brochure which today might be called 'The Care and Feeding of a Vienna Choir Boy' but in 1630 was issued under the prim title of 'Worthy Instructions for the Choirmaster.' Delt with were such matters vital to a boy's well-being as food, sleep, classes, rehearsal, recreation and, of course, prayers. The Hapsburgs liked their choir boys plump, or at least well-fed, for the instructions called for three 'very filling' meals a day with four on fish days. Breakfast was to include a pot of hot soup and each boy was entitled to a loaf of bread a day. Obviously no one was expected to sing on an empty stomach!

Furthermore, wine was to be available with the stipulations that it be wine that would not make anyone ill.

When the Warfield Committee booked the contract for The Vienna Choir Boys for March 7, 1983, from ICM Artists, we were not aware of the widespread popularity of these young singers. The negotiated price was $8,000 (considered a bargain) for one concert. We soon realized that the problem was not as much paying for them as it was seating all those that wanted to come to the concert. However, we did manage to find a seat for everybody, and the evening appeared to be altogether enjoyable for both singers and audience.

VIENNA BOYS CHOIR DRAWS CHEERS

Bravos! Three standing ovations and every seat in the house taken including extra chairs in the orchestra pit! For many years the Vienna Boys have been charming audiences with their concerts.

They did just that last night at Lily Peter Auditorium, singing their hearts out and living up to all expectations with a program of splendid music. They sang with clarity and precision. Considering the ages of 8 to 14, such a performance is more than remarkable and well deserves their reputation of being "one of the oldest musical institutions and one of the youngest and also still the world's best."

In Vienna, the city of song, nearly 500 years ago Emperor Maximilian I founded the Vienna Choir Boys not only to enhance the splendors of the Viennese court but to affirm the glory of God. Many prominent musical careers started with these Austrians. The most famous one was the composer Franz Schubert who was represented on the program here with two selections. "Widerspruch" and "Die Nachtigall," a song with various moods and cadences. Both were delightful to hear.

A strong force in the success of the whole evening was that of conductor Peter Marschik who had a pleasant firmness and rapport with the boys. In addition he proved to be an accomplished pianist in his sparkling and well interpreted accompaniments.

No Viennese program would be complete without hearing from Johann Strauss. The one act opera "Wiener Leben" by Strauss was a humorous and entertaining part of the performance. Leading lady Josephine thrilled the crowd with HIS high clear tones. Composer Strauss was again chosen to conclude the program with a Polka and Waltz the type of music for which he is best known. Two encores added the final and magic touch, "Suzannah" and "Dixie." This affair was sponsored by Warfield Concerts.

—*Helena-West Helena World,* March 8, 1983

Moving on into the prosperous eighties, the reputation of Warfield Concerts continued to grow with favorable recognition. Interest rates on the rise brought more from the Trust which meant better concerts. These were happy times for Warfield Concerts.

Adding to our already extensive list of achievements were performances by Chanticleer, Canadian Brass, the much loved Mantovani Orchestra, and

Metropolitan Opera tenor, James McCracken. The Committee was proud of what had been accomplished.

In May of 1985, I began to feel a few twinges from the seed of thought that Rosalind had left with me years before. There were definite signs, and I understood the message which was *Music Festival.*

The time had come when circumstances were right for us to discuss the possibility of adding a music festival to next year's season. The Committee liked my idea, and we immediately started to make plans.

The Music Festival

The meeting of the Warfield Concerts Committee in May 1985 became historic with the optimistic decision, quickly made, to have a music festival following the 1985-86 regular season. Since then there has been a successful Warfield Music Festival every year, establishing it to be a permanent part of the Warfield Series.

The four members responsible for that decision were: Helen Benton (Mrs. Bill Benton), Cassie Brothers (Mrs. Bill Brothers), and Betty Faust (Mrs. Tom Faust) along with me, who had recently become director emeritus, but continued to be active when needed.

In unhesitating anticipation, we were foolishly credulous in thinking that a music festival would be easy to arrange. Our jubilant naivete was promptly shattered when we began to make plans and realized the magnitude of such an undertaking. Nevertheless, we plunged into preparations with vigor.

Before anything else a date needed to be set, April 27—May 2, 1986, and the fine arts center was engaged for those days.

That being accomplished, the next step started publicity. We had the theme of the festival, *Music in the Air*, printed on hundreds of fliers to introduce the festival. These fliers were printed for us without charge by Lans Hobart, a young man who was working for a small printing business in West Helena known as Fielder's Fast Print. They were mailed in packages to colleges, musical organizations, and various places across the United States where we thought they would arouse interest. At least people were going to know there was a little musical town called Helena, Arkansas.

Gaining confidence with publicity, we daringly put an ad in the big *Musical America* catalog which is printed only once a year and sent all over the world in the early fall about the time new concert seasons begin.

During the hot summer of 1985, concert contracts were completed for six consecutive nights, an accomplishment to be proud of. We had negotiated for reasonable fees but even so the total cost was $26,500. Each presentation was top quality in its field. The variety of artists or groups which had been booked had all received national acclaim, and for our local audiences, there was something to please every taste.

According to Ann Haraway, who made our financial reports, the bank balance on Warfield Concerts was enough to finish the year and have a "carry over" to apply on some of the music festival expenses.

Of course, the yearly allowance from the Warfield Trust could be expected in January. Would that be enough to pay for the remainder of the 1985-86 season, the new fall season, AND the festival? Figures began to dance around in my head, and I wondered.

A sleepless night in September brought to my mind the fact that we were taking too much for granted. Suppose the 1986 allowance was not enough. Suppose there was no "carry over" from 1985. Then what?

Immersed in worries and flashes of doubt, I suddenly had an answer. "When morning comes, I will go out and find sponsors for the festival concerts." I felt reasonably certain that banks or businesses would sponsor a concert in memory of one of their officers.

That sleepless night also gave me another idea. We should have a watercolor exhibition during the festival, an additional feature to attract visitors, one more project for which to find a sponsor.

Before approaching anyone, I called the other committee members who heartily approved. My supposition came true, and within two weeks sponsors were found for each of our concerts.

Helena National Bank was asked to support the watercolor exhibition. Mr. John Robbins, president and chief executive officer, expressed his pleasure and readily agreed to our proposal. He chose to have it called The J.J. White Memorial Watercolor Exhibition in memory of the late Mr. J.J. White, chairman of the board. In addition to his contribution to business, Mr.

White loved art, horticulture, and beautiful things, making it highly appropriate that the exhibition should bear his name.

Stefan Kramar, the famous western artist who is recognized as one the nations top watercolorists, judged the show. He and his wife, Mary, have been favorites in the Mid-South area with their stimulating watercolor workshops.

The social life of the festival started with a remark made to me at church (St. John's Episcopal) one Sunday by Mrs. Jerome Bonaparte Pillow (Cappi) who said, "I would like to give a party during the music festival honoring the patrons." "How wonderful," I replied, "to honor our thoughtful friends who have generously made donations as an expression of appreciation for the free concerts." "Just let me know the day and time," she continued, "and I'll surely do it."

Cappi and Jerome live in one of Helena's most elegant antebellum homes. This Greek Revival mansion was once the home of General James C. Tappan, one of the seven Confederate generals from Phillips County. Union troops used it as their local headquarters during the occupation of Helena, and it is believed that General William T. Sherman quartered in it while in the area. The original kitchen still stands just a few steps from the back of the house.

An imposing two-story residence with a second floor balcony on the front, it is painted pale apricot with white trim. Stately magnolia trees stand on each side of the brick walkway that leads to the porch from a gate of the wrought iron fence surrounding the grounds.

The interior is furnished with authentic antiques once possessed by former members of the family. Ornate silver pieces, the products of silversmiths in the 1880s, grace the banquet table in the dining room, a perfect setting for a party.

Cappi is a charming hostess. She gave a long-to-be-remembered patrons party, our first but not the last. Now, each year we ask someone to have a party for the ever-increasing number of patrons. It is one of the social highlights of the festival.

There were dinners before the concerts and receptions afterward. Helen Benton persuaded her friends to be responsible for these elaborate affairs, which had to include musical entertainment. Even the churches in town presented special music on the opening Sunday. Our *Music in the Air* festival was more than just concerts. The following list shows specifically the unparalleled social life of that week:

FREE CONCERTS - LILY PETER AUDITORIUM - 8 P.M.

APRIL 27, SUNDAY .... Memphis Symphony Orchestra
Alan Balter, conductor
Edwin Hubbard, flutist, guest artist

APRIL 28, MONDAY ...... Metropolitan Opera Soprano .... Gianna Rolandi

APRIL 29, TUESDAY .... Top Brass
A Brass Quintet

APRIL 30, WEDNESDAY .... American Boychoir
26 Voices

MAY 1, THURSDAY .... International Pianist .... Misha Dichter

MAY 2, FRIDAY .... Ballet Arkansas
"The Firebird" and other selections

FREE TICKETS
CHAMBER OF
COMMERCE
P.O. Box 447
Helena. AR 72342
One ticket-
All Concerts

SPECIAL EVENTS

WATERCOLOR EXHIBITION J. J. White Memorial Watercolor Exhibition
Red Room, Phillips County Community College
April 27th - May 2nd, 10 A.M. - 12 Noon - 2 P.M. - 9:30 P.M.

TOURS Historic Homes
Confederate Cemetery
Phillips County Museum
Old Almer Store

SUNDAY, APRIL 27 Opening Ceremony- "Music in the Air"
PCCC campus 5:30 P.M. - 6 P.M.

Starlight Symphony Buffet - 6 P.M. - 7:30 P.M.
PCCC Fine Arts Center
Music by Edwin Hubbard and Combo
Tickets available with reservations.

MONDAY, APRIL 28 Children's Drama "Arkansas Sesquicentennial"
Lily Peter Auditorium, 10 A.M. and 1 P.M.

Seafood Dinner "An Enchanted Evening"
Strolling Violinist
Helena Country Club (open to non-members)
$10.00, 6 P.M. - 7:30 P.M. Cash Bar
Reservations Required

TUESDAY, APRIL 29 Helena-New Orleans style supper
Mikes Place - Cherry street
"River City Six" - Dixieland Jazz Band
$10.00, 4:30 P.M. - 7:30 P.M.

WEDNESDAY, APRIL 30 Chamber of Commerce Luncheon - visitors invited
Music will be provided

THURSDAY, MAY 1 Pre-Concert party honoring Warfield patrons
Mr. and Mrs. Jerome B. Pillow - 715 Poplar - Helena - 6 P.M.

FRIDAY, MAY 2 Arkansas Day
Schedule to be announced.

Early spring of 1986. We knew the time had come to finalize every detail. Up to that point, decorations had not been discussed.

Gloria Higginbottom of Marvell, a personable

young woman who had developed a talent for decorating and party giving, was called. Meeting with us briefly, she was employed to beautify the stage, the lobby, and dining hall. "We are leaving this entirely in your hands," she was told. "Make everything pretty and unusual." That she did.

S.D. Warfield stage was lavishly dressed with masses of fresh flowers and greenery, a loan from Watson's Florist (through the years Frances and Watson Light have often kindly allowed us to borrow their graceful ferns and other plants). The emerald radiance of the leaves was effectively illuminated by tiny lights that magically twinkled among them, an eye-catching sight as people began to fill the auditorium. After the festival ended, Watson's Flowers and Gifts received a letter of appreciation from the Warfield Committee thanking them for the continual generosity with their florals.

In the lobby, Gloria used mirrors and heavy silver paper on the walls. A long table she covered in black with brass ornaments creating a decidedly stylized and sophisticated effect one might expect to find in New York City not in a southern river town of more than one hundred fifty years. But it was surprisingly different and brought on plenty of comments and small talk from those who were smitten by this new concept in decor.

The reception hall was transformed into a virtual garden. Making use of varieties of iris and flowering shrubs in seasonal bloom all over town she had multi-colored bouquets on each table and wicker floor baskets filled with the same flowers standing at vantage points in the room. Adding to the garden-like appearance were huge wooden washtubs holding young trees. These like the stage greenery glittered with little lights.

Typical of Mississippi Delta party-giving, white lattice trimmed with ivy was placed around the side of the hall to disguise some of the starkness of the concrete walls of the building.

Sunday afternoon, April 27, 1986—our opening date—arrived. Months before, when I assumed the responsibility of the opening ceremony, I was free to put my heart into it. Since the fall of 1985, I had indefatigably focused my energy on making the festival an outstanding success. In my wildest dreams, I had reveled in the thought that it would be similar to the annual Spoleto Festival in Charleston, South Carolina. Only in dreams could that be—particularly in view of our limited assets, lack of funds, inexperience, and a much smaller community. What we did have were good friends who untiringly worked to help us make it a thoroughly delightful event, one which gave our area a cultural boost.

For me, my joyful expectations to be involved in the happenings of that special week were suddenly taken away. A month before the festival Winston became seriously ill with kidney failure. One of his kidneys had been removed several years before. He was taken to the Baptist Hospital in Memphis where surgery was immediately performed to remove an aneurysm pressing on the kidney. The surgeons felt that relieving the pressure would allow normal functioning. It did little good, and Winston remained in intensive care until his death.

I tried to carry on my duties at home and be in Memphis at the same time. Back and forth, I went under extreme pressure. Suddenly the day before the music festival, Winston became very much better, and I felt confident enough to come home to do the opening ceremony as planned.

At 5:30 P.M. on Sunday, a crowd of all ages gathered outside the fine arts center. The sun shone brightly in a cloudless sky, and a gentle breeze cooled the atmosphere as if to say "summer is not yet here."

Dr. Eleanor Pietch, head of the music department at Phillips County Community College, served as mistress of ceremonies. Father Tom Marks gave the invocation. Patriotic music was performed by the Central High School band directed by Jerry Rains, and the choral groups from Central High and from the College were directed by Dennis Burton.

Nearly everyone joined in singing "The Star Spangled Banner" and "A Mighty Fortress is Our God." Next on the program was music to "A Litany for America" with narration by Dr. Pietch.

Concluding the ceremony one thousand balloons

bearing the words, MUSIC IN THE AIR, were released. Credit for the balloon finale goes to George James and his printing company. He not only gave us the balloons but brought them to the ceremony packed in his truck and opened the door at exactly the right minute for them to sail in the air. It was an emotion-rousing display. I often wondered where they went. As far as I know, not a single balloon was ever seen again.

We moved into the dining hall for the gala dinner with Edwin Hubbard's Combo playing favorite tunes. Blanche Choate, (Mrs. Tom Choate), acting as hostess, welcomed the guests as they entered. She had been completely in charge of the dinner and had capably worked out every detail of this sumptuous affair.

I had time to serve myself from the buffet table of gorgeous food when a message came for me to come to the door. My heart sank. I seemed to know. The word was Winston had suddenly died.

Gloria and Gene, my daughter and son-in-law, were there. They took me home. As far as I was concerned the music festival had come abruptly to an end. Winston's funeral was held Tuesday at twelve noon at St. John's Episcopal Church and was conducted by the Reverend Duane Saba; the service was touching, and the music was beautiful. The choir was largely increased in numbers by some of my musical friends from other churches. It was their way of showing me that they cared.

Eleanor and Dennis

My friendship with Eleanor and Dennis has brought many sunny moments in my life. Especially have I loved their music, both sacred and secular, which has been generously shared with others.

The rich warm tones of Dennis Burton's extraordinarily beautiful tenor voice can soften a heart of stone. Using perfect diction, he sings with natural ease no matter how much volume may be necessary. His voice is best described as being quite similar to Placido Domingo's. Both began their careers as baritones but developed a tenor quality and range.

Seated at a majestic pipe organ, her auburn hair gleaming in the light like freshly polished copper, Eleanor, known to her students as Dr. Eleanor E. Pietch, was at her best. She filled the hall or sanctuary with brilliant sound. If the mood changed, she could produce light lyrical passages floating in the air, music that soothed the emotions of the listeners. When accompanying a soloist or choral group, Eleanor was intensely sensitive to tempo and volume support needed by the performer. No doubt, she was a talented accompanist.

In spite of a lengthy span of years between our ages, I have had a lasting acquaintance with both Eleanor and Dennis. They are in the younger end of the same generation as my children and some of my appreciation may bear a tinge of motherly instinct. I have enjoyed their ambitious challenges and am proud of their achievements. I confess that occasionally I have been the one who created a challenge.

Such was the case when Dennis and Eleanor appeared in a vocal and organ recital as one of the concerts during a Warfield Music Festival. The date was April 30, 1989.

I first knew Dennis soon after he and his wife, Becky, arrived here more than twenty years ago. Dennis was just out of college. They made a striking couple. Becky's dark hair, blue eyes, and middle height contrasted with Dennis' light-brown hair, blue eyes, and six-feet-four stature.

Becky quickly received a position at Merchants and Farmers Bank, while Dennis assumed the duties of choral director at Central High School. He also became a member of a small group of chosen singers in the Holiday Choir of Temple Beth El where I had been singing for several years. To me, it was a privilege to be a part of that ecumenical choir. The presence of Dennis and his powerful voice gave us a lift.

Right away, I realized how much it would mean if he would join the choir at St. John's. I am delighted to write that our tenor said "yes" to my persuasion and encouragement. Thus, he became an important part of our church music. In addition to singing, he is now choir director, standing before us with graying hair and a well-trimmed gray beard which gives evidence of the passing years. Further proof of time and change are his two fine boys, Jason, 18, and Colin, 14. Both have inherited musical talents that promise notable vocal careers.

Dennis and his Central High School choirs have amazed audiences by their pure tones and flawless performances, exceptional for students of high school level. They have continually received state honors, and several times his Meistersingers have been heard at Carnegie Hall. Dennis himself is esteemed by his peers and has acquired a reputation as a distinguished conductor and educator. Presently he is Arkansas State President of the American Choral Directors Association and in 1996 was voted Director of the Year. My visions of Dennis taking bows from the stage of the Metropolitan Opera Company did not materialize. He definitely had the talent to pursue such a forceful course, but he loved his family and was satisfied with what he was doing.

Originally from Lorain, Ohio, Eleanor was a graduate of Arizona State University where she received her doctorate in organ performance. She was proud of her degree, and it pleased her to be referred to as Dr. Eleanor E. Pietch. She signed a contract to head the music department at Phillips County Community College which brought her to Helena in August 1984 to make her home.

Eleanor was energetic, strong, and almost overly zealous in doing her work. Eager to establish a favorable place in our community, she welcomed additional jobs.

One of them was to be organist and choir director at St. John's Church, a rather difficult spot for a newcomer facing a small choir consisting mainly of older singers who had been there for years.

Instead of being discouraged, she managed to add some new members from her choral groups at the college. For Christmas, Easter, and other special church celebrations requiring a large choir, Eleanor could "round up" enough temporary singers to fill our needs. Inspired by extra help, we would sing such glorious anthems as Handel's *Hallelujah Chorus*, Gounod's *Sanctus,* or *Gloria in Excelsis* from Mozart's 12th Mass.

I think the finest moments of her career during the five years she lived here were the performances of the Warfield Concerts Chorale. They belonged to Eleanor—they were some of the stars in her dreams. The Warfield Committee needed a Christmas concert in 1986. We contacted Eleanor who agreed to organize and conduct a large choral group chosen from local choirs and those in the surrounding area, particularly Little Rock and Marianna. A final count amounted to almost sixty persons, who resolutely promised faithful attendance at every rehearsal. She employed 12 competent instrumentalists from the Arkansas Symphony Orchestra to accompany them.

Eleanor worked tirelessly through the fall of that year. When inclement weather prohibited out-of-town people from attending a practice, she would drive to Little Rock the next night and give those in that area a special rehearsal. Nothing was too much trouble to make the Warfield Chorale the very best.

On opening night, her decided individualism came alive when Eleanor did not conduct in one of the usual black robes worn by the singers. Instead, she wore a custom-made evening gown of her own original design. As the spotlight pointed to the conductor's entrance, Eleanor gracefully floated out to the podium in a long dress of black lace over pink silk. Margaret Mitchell's Scarlett would have liked that dress to charm Rhett Butler. Her full skirt supported underneath by crinoline puffed out from the tight bodice. She was lovely to see, and the concert was magnificent.

In the next two years, 1987 and 1988, Eleanor gave us superb Christmas concerts with the Warfield Chorale. For each performance, she wore an exquisite new gown; one had been made of bright green iridescent taffeta draped in the back to form a bustle, and the other of black satin, displaying long panels of sequins.

No more Warfield Chorale concerts. In June 1989

Eleanor moved to Huntsville, Alabama, to teach in a four-year college. I grieved over her departure. Through our church choir and our mutual love of music, Eleanor and I had become devoted friends. With her doing the driving, we attended out-of-town concerts and shopping trips to Memphis. She often helped me with my duties at home. I can remember one snowy day when Eleanor shoveled the snow off my driveway. She gave useful gifts to my grandchildren and occasionally sent flowers. Most of all, we loved to talk about music.

I am sorry to relate that she suddenly died in June 1991. Her death was attributed to brain hemorrhage. How sad for her young life to be over. I have missed my dear friend.

Tempus Fugit

Tempus Fugit, that inevitable passing of time from one year to another, when the rising and setting sun turns days into months and months into years. We are acclimatized to the perpetual changing of seasons, and we know that every twelfth month a new calendar must be hung on the wall.

Time moves on leaving multi-colored memories, some long-to-be-cherished, other wishing to be forgotten.

With the opening of the 1992-93 season of Warfield Concerts, time had left us twenty-five years of musical memories, performances, and concerts varying in type and merit the majority of which were deservedly classical.

Such a momentous milestone gave cause for a special quarter-century celebration. We thoroughly agreed to that, but working out the details required time-consuming consultations, telephone calls, and compromises.

Decision number one was not difficult. The Memphis Symphony Orchestra had played for the first ever Warfield Concert and was the natural choice for the one commemorating twenty-five years.

Matching a date when the symphony could play with a time the Lily Peter Auditorium could be used became a perplexing matter.

Because of specific contracts with guest artists and definite rehearsal schedules, the symphony's few "run out" performances had to be made either preceding or immediately following a Memphis concert weekend. Their concert weekends were planned a year or more in advance.

Under the direction of Mr. Kirk Whiteside, the Drama Department of Phillips County Community College had developed to the extent of having exclusive use of the S.D. Warfield stage for an entire month to do a production.

A conversation with Mr. Ron Jewel, manager of Memphis Symphony, informed us of their chosen date for a Helena performance: February 2, 1993.

To do his musical, Kirk Whiteside told us he needed the entire month, and seemed unyielding to any schedule changes.

Both Ron and Kirk are gentlemen of the theater, and their multifarious talents are revealed in different ways. Ron, an agreeable person in his early forties, is about five feet ten inches and has thick, long blonde hair, which touches the tops of his ears. He also possesses a well-trimmed mustache. When he colors his hair gray and dons a mustache, eye-glasses, white suit and small black tie, he bears striking resemblance to that famous author of *Life on the Mississippi*. In fact, his calendar is filled with Mark Twain appearances in the south.

Kirk is a genuinely cordial young man, slender and medium in height. He has brown hair, pleasant eyes, and a superlative speaking voice, which is a priceless asset for the stage. The deep resonance of his voice is smooth and deep, like a piece of rich velvet.

Being the one who was doing the necessary negotiations for Warfield Concerts, I became the go-between, feeling as if I were entangled in a maze of challenging obstacles with nothing but my persuasive powers to work through them. FINALLY, Ron and Kirk decided to engage in serious conversation, resulting in the Memphis Symphony Orchestra agreeing to the date of Saturday, January 30, 1993, for the anniversary concert. What a relief to have our major problem settled, even if it would be almost a year before this prestigious concert took place. There was certainly time to anticipate the event.

Later on, when definite plans were shaping up, I was utterly surprised and pleased beyond measure to be included in the celebration. The January concert and the reception which followed was dedicated in my honor, and recognized my twenty-five years of service on the Warfield Committee.

In Celebration and Appreciation

The concert tonight is celebrating the Twenty-Fifth Anniversary of Warfield Concerts and honoring Helen Mosby. The first Warfield Concert was in 1968 at Central High School Gymnasium with the Memphis Symphony Orchestra performing. It is both fitting and proper that the Memphis Symphony be performing again for Warfield Concerts on this special occasion.

Mrs. Mosby is being honored for having served on the original Warfield Concerts Committee that was formed in 1967. It is with both joy and gratitude that we honor Helen Mosby tonight; joy for the pleasure that she has brought to music lovers throughout this area and gratitude for her service, dedication, and guidance on the Warfield Concerts Committee.

I was deeply touched and of course excited, but above all, I was and still am eternally grateful for one of the finest experiences of my life, one which will be to the end of my days a treasured memory. Once again, I thank everyone who had a part in it.

For me, the concert and party were matchless perfection. Preceding the program dressed in my favorite evening gown, a bodice of black velvet with a black fox collar and a voluminous red satin skirt, I was presented with an enchanting bouquet of flowers, which I carried during the reception.

The hall glowed with lights, a table of food dressed in a lace cloth and centered with a large array of blossoms, and people laughing and talking in a spirit of gaiety, especially in the abundant graciousness of my friends. From beginning to the end the evening was one of supreme pleasure.

HONORS HELEN P. MOSBY

Warfield Concerts celebrates 25th

The Twenty-fifth Anniversary Season of Warfield Concerts was celebrated in grand style Saturday night with a performance of the Memphis Symphony Orchestra.

This quarter-of-a-century of concerts began on the night of April 22, 1968 when a smaller, but very good, Memphis Symphony Orchestra conducted by Vincent de Frank played for the first Warfield Concert. The guest artist was violinist Young Uck Kim playing Saint Saens *Concerto #3* for violin and orchestra. The concert was held in the old gymnasium at Central High School before an audience consisting for the most part of S.D. Warfield's loyal friends.

Time has been kind. The concert seasons have grown and improved. There are larger audiences, operas, ballets, big names and best of all the wonderful S.D. Warfield Memorial Stage in the Lily Peter Auditorium at the Fine Arts Center of the Phillips County Community College. Seventy members of the Memphis Symphony conducted by Alan Balter were assembled together Saturday night. This time the guest artist was Max Huls, their concert master.

Before the music started Mrs. Dick Hendrix, a Warfield Committee member, made a few appropriate remarks from the stage. She welcomed everyone to this special occasion including the announcement that the concert and reception afterward were in honor of Helen Mosby for her 25 years of service on the Warfield Concerts Committee.

Lights dimmed, the musicians prepared for the downbeat, and the large audience burst into applause as Maestro Balter came on stage. Before stepping on the podium he also spoke briefly to the audience, expressing his appreciation and that of the orchestra for being a part of the 25th anniversary celebration.

Alan Balter has received national acclaim as a conductor. He is energetic, he is sensitive to deep levels of interpretation, and he extends a friendliness and warmth from the podium that greatly pleases his audiences.

The program opened with Trojan March from the opera, *Les Troyens* by Hector Berlioz, a composer of the true Romantic period. This vigorous, fantastic march used full orchestra. The brasses accented the rhythmic patterns of the piece as the music moved rapidly along to a brilliant conclusion.

This lively piece was followed by the delicate tones of Felix Mendelssohn's *Concerto in E Minor for Violin and Orchestra Op.64*, one of the most melodious and lovable of his works. Mendelssohn designated that the three movements be played without pause. After a brief orchestral introduction in the first movement, solo violinist Max Huls introduced the principal melody, first softly then soaring to passionate beauty. The Andante brought out a second melody, but the principal theme frequently appeared between orchestra and soloist. Lyric cadenzas and difficult virtuostic passages were performed with impressive accuracy by Mr. Huls who received tremendous applause and a standing ovation.

After intermission the orchestra played a beautiful *Symphony in D Minor Op. 70* by Antonin Dvorak. It opened solemnly with a subject in the lower strings followed by tender moments, dramatic passages, and a chorale for woodwinds. The finale, however, was both solemn and agitated. This marvelous work by Dvorak was a magnificent conclusion to a wonderful concert which by many music lovers will be long and fondly remembered.

Following the concert Phillips County Community College and the Warfield Concerts Committee invited the entire orchestra and audience to a lovely reception in the Community Room.

— *Daily World,* February 1, 1993

Quotations

While working on our twenty-fifth anniversary programs, it seemed fitting to say something about S.D. Warfield in addition to the perennial paragraph under his picture that appears regularly inside the cover.

The idea came to me to include in the program for that season brief quotations from his friends. Some had died and others moved out-of-town, but there were enough of us who still had friendly affectionate memories of him to fill three pages in the program.

Printers have been known to make forgivable errors. This happened to the quote by Mr. Robert M. (Bob) Hornor, Jr., a long-time intimate friend of S.D. Bob's whole family, his grandmother known as Miss Fannie Mae, mother, father and sister always welcomed D. as they would a member of their own family.

Mr. Hornor's quote was inadvertently omitted. I record it now as follows.

S.D. Warfield—a Southern gentleman who left for all time a very unique and wonderful heritage and gift.

—Bob Hornor, past member,
Warfield Concerts Committee

Bob Hornor was a valuable member of the Warfield Committee, serving for six years from 1974 through 1979. He had the astuteness to make wise decisions quickly and intelligently and the ability to move forward and accomplish his intentions. He supported me in the work I was trying to do, for which I am grateful.

Bob Hornor, tall, gray hair, and blue eyes is now a distinguished gentleman in his mid-sixties. He is busy with extensive farming interests but finds time to assume responsibilities at St. John's Church. He was married to the late Janice Kurts. His two step-daughters are Dana, living in Helena with Bob, and Lisa, owner and operator of a fascinating art gallery in Memphis. His loyalty to our community never wavers.

25 YEARS OF WARFIELD
CONCERTS WITH MEMORIES OF S.D.

"I remember S.D. as a lively and charming Southern gentleman in a white suit whose positive outlook shone through his smiling blue eyes. No matter how good I felt, he always made me feel better ... and because of his lasting legacy of music, he still does."

—Tene Nichols

"Samuel Drake Warfield more than anyone else, took us in mind and spirit far from Helena to that world at large, a knowledge of which makes us all the more fondly aware of whence we come."

—George E.N. de Man, Atlanta, Georgia

"Through his generous legacy, S.D. enriched our lives immeasurably, bringing the world of music to our doorstep."

—Christine Heslep Coates

"He was a lifelong friend."

—Jane Pillow Rightor Lee-Mclean, Virginia

"S.D. had a great zest for life."

—Virginia Mosby LeMaistre, Tuscaloosa, Alabama

"If I were asked for a definition of 'Savoire Faire' I should simply say ... D. Warfield."

—Allen Keesee

"People have asked if we were close friends of D. I reckon so! He was a member of the wedding party of every member of both of our families."
—Francis Miles Keesee

"D. was 'un Monsieur Tres Elegant."
—Mimi and Nunzio Messina

"Civic Music Concerts, Methodist, Episcopal and Temple Beth El Choirs, the Melody Club and other musical groups helped influence S.D. to leave us this wonderful gift."
—Doc and Sara Baker

"He was a true and loyal friend and we all miss him."
—Frank A. Jeffett, Dallas, Texas

"D. was one of my favorite relatives. He gave me much good advice when I was growing up."
—Margaret Gist Watson, Columbus, Georgia

"My visits to Helena, that friendly Seaport City, were made even more pleasant by knowing S.D. Warfield, a delightful gentleman of the Old South."
—Johnnye Catherine Polk Rinker, Denver, Colorado

"Not only did S.D. 'hand pick' each flower for each person to suit the personality ..: he had a special interest in Lanie's piano playing and was an inspiration to her ...."
—Frances and Watson Light

"I am so glad I had the privilege of knowing him and being his friend. I am doubly thankful now because of his wonderful contribution to this community."
—Lorena Connaway

"Three generations of our family were enriched by his friendship and loyalty."   —Katherine Hill

"S.D. was a friend to all ages of people."
—Elizabeth "Libby" Polk Wolf

"D. had more than one love. He loved to dance and dance he did."   —Katy Miller

"When remembering D. we recall gracious evenings of lovely music. How fortunate we are to be the recipients of that legacy."   —David and Miriam Solomon

"After making S.D. the mold was broken."
—Gene and Glen Orr, Jacksonville, Florida

"Ole Miss, good music, and the people of Phillips County.... S.D. loved all three ... and so do we."
—Bettye and Dick Hendrix

"D. was an elegant friend. We had many happy times dancing together. I am pleased to be part of a page in his honor as he was an important part of my life growing up."
—Marguerite Hornor Gist, Carrollton, Georgia

"His cheerfulness and enthusiasm brightened many occasions."

—Gloria Polk Nobles, Memphis

"When you danced with S.D., you felt like Ginger Rogers."

—Edwynne Gordon Cooper, McAllen, Texas

"He was a wonderful friend of my entire family."

—Margaret Hoskins Bush

"His unique personality gave us many surprises."

—Janet and Myron Schrantz

"I remember S.D. as the very essence of the perfect 'Southern Gentleman' not to mention the best dancer in Arkansas."

—Nita Anderson, Memphis

"The gift of music that S.D. left to Helena and the surrounding communities is a treasure for which all of us should be forever grateful."

—Woodfin Keesee, Mt. Kisco, New York

"S.D. ... an ageless Southern Gentleman who left a marvelous legacy for the benefit of all .... He escorted my mother in the twenties and thirties, my cousin in the forties, me in the fifties, and my sister in the sixties. He loved music, parties, dancing and particularly cauliflower."

—Frances Curtis Howe, Knoxville, Tennessee

"The epitome of sophistication ... an educated profile outside and above the schoolroom was Samuel Drake Warfield."

—William T. Tappan, Sr. Corrales, New Mexico

"He loved the Cherry St. coffee crowd. At 10 A.M., we could always expect him, arriving in his black Chevrolet."   —Clancy King

"We never even considered S.D. was like Fred Astaire. We thought Fred Astaire was amazingly like S.D.— truly elegant."

—Cappi and Jerome Pillow

"S.D. and I shared a friendship that was heightened by our mutual interest in the music of the United Methodist Church. His love for the works of Gounod and particularly for the solo, 'O Divine Redeemer' stand out in my memories of him."

—Emma Lee Gordon

"S.D. seemed to grow up anew with each succeeding Helena generation. When our turn came he provided my first experience of what I then considered a true sophisticate—a 'man of the world' with a genuine zest for life. How wonderful to have this living legacy through his concert series."

—Maratha Brewer Rhodes, Osceola, Arkansas

"God's blessings on Samuel Drake. His descriptive remark on a hot summer day was, "I feel like I am simmering in my own juice."
—W.R. Bob Orr, Salt Lake City, Utah

"A loyal Methodist and Sunday School Treasurer, S.D.'s favorite anthem was Gounod's 'Sanctus.'"
—June Gayle Haraway

"We own a sterling silver candle snuffer which was his signature wedding gift."
—Al Haraway

"S.D. Warfield was my patient and good friend who is greatly missed."
—Dr. C.M.T. Kirkman

"I am deeply grateful for the joy I have experienced in serving on the Warfield Concert Committee for twenty-five years and knowing that S.D.'s bounteous gift will continue to illuminate the cultural aspects of this community."
—Helen Polk Mosby

Honored

My immediate family is a medley of various ages and genders, all genuinely concerned about my well-being. They were aware of my advancing age, or more often called declining years, and decided to sponsor a Warfield Concert in my honor, an act which will remain a treasured memory as long as I live.

Of my seven family members were my oldest daughter, Gloria Polk Nobles, and her two adult daughters, Helen Polk Nobles and Lillian (Lil) Lobdell Nobles, my younger daughter, Elizabeth "Libby" Polk Wolf, and her two teenage children, Clopton Wolf (age 14), and his younger sister Polk Wolf (age 12), and Catherine Polk MacAdam, the daughter of my oldest child, Cad L. Polk, III, who died in 1991 at the age of 59.

The frequency of the name Polk is understandable. They are the children and grandchildren of my first husband, the late Cadwallader Leonidas Polk, Jr. What a long name, but it carries a certain cadence, and I jokingly have said to him, "Your name reminds me of a Latin declension," recalling the Latin grammar classes in high school when we were made to decline nouns and conjugate verbs. To family and friends that long name became Cad, although he was always proud of his middle name coming from his great uncle, the fighting Bishop Leonidas Polk of Civil War history.

By profession, Cad was an attorney, serving as city attorney and deputy prosecuting attorney along with his private practice. He also held the position of president of the Helena-West Helena School Board for twenty years before his untimely death in an automobile accident on the night of Friday, October 13, 1950. The tragedy was caused by two men who were driving while intoxicated. Shortly before the accident, they had been arrested by the Forrest City, Arkansas, police. Instead of holding them, they were fined $10 and released. Then, they ran head-on into our car as we were returning with Gloria and two other band students from a Central High School football game at Brinkley, Arkansas. Gloria's two friends were not injured, but she and I were critical. I was in and out of hospitals for the following six months. In time, we both recovered completely.

In spite of being the tallest girl (5'8") in my graduating class (1927), I had a pleasant social life with many agreeable friends. Still, I longed to be small and have people say, "Helen Clopton is a 'cute blonde.'" I would gladly have exchanged my dark hair and brown eyes for blue eyes and blond curls. With these disturbing thoughts, I planned a future.

My husband must be short so our children would be boys six feet tall with my genes. Our girls would be short inheriting his lack of height. The idea materialized to some extent but not completely.

Cad, blue eyes and blond curly hair that disappeared on top as he grew older, became my husband soon after I returned home from two years away at school. He was not quite my height which did not hinder the joy we had in sharing our fondness for music, dancing, parties, and the choir at St. John's Church. We were happily compatible.

Then came young Cad III, a bright mind that made National Honor Society, played football, an acolyte in the church. He did what he was supposed to do except inherit my tall genes. In maturity he was the same size as his father, but his accomplishments and personality overshadowed any absence of inches.

Gloria arrived four years later. Surprisingly, it was little four-year-old Cad, who named her in this way. He was brought to the hospital to see the new baby. At first glance he innocently burst forth with the words, "Glory Hallelujah! My sister's here." That was a clue. We named her Gloria, a name seeming just right as her personality developed.

Her brown eyes twinkled with animation and good spirit. She is blessed with unlimited energy. My "plan" had worked. Gloria measured 5'2" and occasionally in her younger days was called "cute." She is an achiever who thrives on challenges like being valedictorian and later Phi Beta Kappa at Vanderbilt University. She is married to Dr. Eugene R. Nobles. Living in Memphis, she enjoys the activities of her girls. Life continues to give Gloria many challenges.

Libby was my war-baby, born December 1944, during those unsettled World War II years when mothers lost sons and families lost fathers, a time that tested our patriotism and willingness to sacrifice. Sugar, butter, gasoline, and other necessities were rationed. Sulfanilamide, a colorless sulfonamide drug with antibacterial properties, came into use. It was followed by penicillin. We called them the miracle drugs. The first nylon stockings appeared in shops. Heavy and unflattering to legs, their good quality was the durability to wear on and on without a hole or run.

My "plan" for girls fell by the way with Libby who became the tallest member of the family, standing five-feet-ten and one-half inches. Her brown eyes, brown curly hair, and delicate features make her a pretty person. She and I find it convenient to be tall, particularly when shopping for clothes. We are easy to fit. We are called on to reach things from shelves or replace light bulbs in the ceiling, and are always glad to be helpful.

Libby is proud of her two children. Clopton, a brunette who resembles his mother, is growing taller every day. Polk (we call her Polky) is easily recognized by her abundance of long red hair. Her fair skin makes it necessary to dodge the sunshine, a handicap, because she is quite athletic. She too is pretty. Both children make As in school, and Libby is ambitious for their futures. Presently, they live in Helena with me.

The oldest of the grandchildren is Cathy, an attractive and intelligent young woman with dark hair and big blues eyes. She is married to Donald MacAdam. They have two little ones, Donnie Polk MacAdam and baby Catherine Elizabeth Polk MacAdam. California is their home, but every Christmas the MacAdams visit me.

My namesake, Helen Polk Nobles, is my size and has my coloring. She is a registered nurse with a B.S. in nursing from Vanderbilt University. Helen has a wholesome enthusiasm and kindness in her nature, which is a gift that gives comfort to others. She is now married to Christopher Bird, but she plans to continue in her nursing profession—at least for a while.

Lil, a vivacious little blonde, surprises people with her talents. She always has excelled in her studies, and in the business world she has displayed a determination of purpose and desire for accomplishment. Lil is presently in pharmaceutical sales for Abbott Laboratories, enjoying the freedom of her work and the contact with many interesting new friends.

The first steps toward arranging a family-sponsored concert were consultations among themselves. I was included in the discussions, more telephone calls than meetings, concerning prices, artists, and dates. Surely I did not want this much-anticipated event to be a financial burden on anyone. Therefore, I persisted in reminding them that perfectly desirable performances were available at a cost of about $2,000. That information brought about a quick and easy decision to engage the Guild Trio from Joanne Rile Management Company for a concert on Wednesday, September 28, 1994.

The Guild Trio is composed of pianist Patricia Tao, violinist Janet Orenstein, and cellist Brooks Whitehouse. Ms. Orenstein and Mr. Whitehouse are husband and wife. All three are soloists of international fame. Since its formation in 1988, when they merged their individual talents, this trio of gifted artists has received critical acclaim both at home and abroad.

The concert was beautiful in every sense of the word, displaying delicately rhythmical passages and powerfully moving crescendos. Their interpretive insight of the four movements of Beethoven's "Archduke Trio" made it my favorite piece on the program. The open delight these young players had in making music was obvious to the listeners who were charmed by what they heard. It was my pleasure to honor The Guild Trio with a reception at my home after the performance. Years of Warfield Concerts have made me realize that people in the audience welcome the chance for a personal word or two with the artist. For that reason, we have entertained as often as possible after the concerts.

In negotiating for Warfield Concerts, sometimes we could get the performance fee reduced if room and board were furnished, which is what happened in signing the contract for The Guild Trio. My warmhearted friend Betty Faust kindly offered to meet the trio at the Memphis Airport and bring them to her home to visit while they were here.

Betty and her husband, Tom, have reared four children in their comfortable home, a handsome house built of cypress on Stonebrook Road, where guests are welcome and graciously treated (I hope the trio appreciated her hospitality). Betty remembers the look of surprise when she brought them inside and they saw the wide range of the entrance hall opening into an oversize living room having a vaulted ceiling with exposed cypress beams and a heavy stone fireplace. Realizing the good acoustics therein, cellist Whitchouse quickly exclaimed, "I bid to practice here!" Turning to the other two Betty said, "There's lots more space. Try my huge recreation area on the lower level." Betty's house is serviceable and conveniently arranged for company. Our musicians would be well-cared-for, including some good southern cooking.

Our next problem was finding a way for them to go back to the Memphis Airport the morning after the concert. The startling part of this undertaking was the fact that their flight left at 7 A.M. making it necessary to leave here at five. Who in the world would be willing to drive them at that unearthly hour?

We managed to engage Woodie Cook, one of the retired gentlemen in town, who, for something to do, drives elderly people when they go out-of-town to doctors, shopping, or to the airport. Woodie is pleasant, dependable, and an excellent driver. He is in great demand. My car was to be used for the trip.

Woodie's own words can better describe his experience: "I decided to go to the concert and reception the night before to soak up a little classical music and pick up a few ideas for conversation with the artists. It was hard to sleep that night for fear I would not be on time. But at 5 A.M., I was waiting at the Faust house in Helen Mosby's car.

"The one who played the piano sat in the front seat with me. The cello and luggage went into the trunk. Miss Orenstein insisted on keeping the violin with her on the floor of the backseat. We arrived promptly at the airport. I stopped in front of the right entrance to unload. While they got out of the car, I removed everything from the trunk. There they stood with their belongings thanking me and saying goodbye. I wished them well, got in the car, and drove directly home."

Before Woodie reached my house Betty called me. "You won't believe this. Janet Orenstein has just telephoned from Nashville where their plane made a short stop. She left her violin on the floor of the car."

"Oh, my goodness! What are we going to do?" I replied.

Betty continued, "She said to pack the violin in a box that does not look like a violin. Then send it by UPS insured for only $25,000, although its real value runs into six figures."

"Then why so little?" I asked.

"Because heavily insured would arouse suspicion and it might be stolen."

We followed her instructions. Never have I packed anything as carefully. Fortunately for us Woodie had to make another trip to Memphis the next day to take Mr. Gibson Turley to the doctor. They would both be glad to take the violin and mail it.

With Mr. Turley along, I felt confident. He was a prominent citizen, highly successful in business and efficient in anything he undertook. Together he and Woodie would let nothing go awry.

The last call from Janet came the next day. "The violin is safely in my hands. Please thank Woodie and give him $15 for his trouble."

For Betty and me it was RELIEF.

Two B's and a C

The social and leadership personalities of Betty, Bettye, and Cassie compliment each other as effectively as the sides of an equilateral triangle. All three are workers who are dedicated and willing to make sacrifices for the benefit of their common goal, the Warfield Concerts.

Composing the present Warfield Concerts Committee are: Betty Faust (Mrs. Tom Faust), Bettye Hendrix (Mrs. Dick Hendrix), and Cassie Brothers (Mrs. Bill Brothers).

Concert Committees try to please the public with an enjoyable and interesting assortment of programs, but at times they unhappily have to smile through criticism when a concert has not been what was expected. Individuals in the audience do not hesitate to express displeasure if a performance is not to their liking.

Remarks can be heard: "Too loud!" "I couldn't hear a word he said." "Frozen! I feel like the iceberg that sunk the Titanic." "I'm suffocating in this place." "Nice concert but too long. Should have stopped at intermission." "Guess it was good but too high class for me." "Did you like that freakish costume?" "That man in front of me wobbles his head. I wish to heavens he would settle on one spot."

In contrast, and much more frequently, compliments abound: "Wonderful! I could just sit back down and hear that whole symphony again." "I loved every minute." "The staging was spectacular." "This marvelous production should please everyone." "Did you see those hands flying up and down the keyboard? He did not miss a single note. Perfect touch." "Her top tone must have been a clear high C." "Those Russians can surely sing and all of it *a cappella*!" "This was an excellent presentation of the *Nutcracker*. Wish we could have it every year." "May I go back and get his autograph?"

After a particularly grueling night with all kinds of mishaps behind the scenes, these expressive phrases of approbation provide a degree of comfort to the tired spirits of the committee.

One thing that can always be counted on is plenty of applause from the audience. Even if not excited or thrilled over the concert, they dutifully clap, and if the artist appears appreciative, a standing ovation will take place. We have been criticized for encouraging too many standing ovations. Some say only a top performance should receive such spontaneous acclaim. Personally, I do not think it does any harm to make a performer feel well-received, and consequently leave town liking us. Through my many conversations with booking agents all over the country, I know Warfield Concerts have acquired a reputation for cordiality and thoughtful attentions to the visiting artists. They are heartily welcomed. We have made a good reputation for our town.

Few people have any conception of the demands experienced by Warfield Committee members. They are approached with requests for certain concerts from those who do not understand that artists have to be touring in our direction to make a stop here. Telephone calls and more telephone calls take place to complete a contract. Papers are mailed back and forth for signatures, and just as is seems finished with everything in place, some unexpected circumstance can upset the diligently prepared agreement. Then, a new start has to be made, resulting in an entirely different concert from the one previously attempted.

A never-to-be-forgotten experience happened a few years ago when a group of singers from Little Rock, Arkansas, scheduled to perform on Sunday afternoon February 9, 1992, called two hours before the concert to say, "We can't come. The bus driver has disappeared." What a blow! It was a cold winter day, but standing in front of Lily Peter Auditorium to tell people arriving for the concert to turn around and go home kindled in our body a warmth that dissipated any sensation of cold.

So far, that has been a one and only time for which we had to thank our lucky stars. I fervently hope

Zodiac's Aquarius will stay in a good humor from now on.

Betty Faust is currently handling contract negotiations and writing newspaper publicity for the immediate committee. A Phi Beta Kappa graduate of the University of Arkansas, she is eminently qualified for both of these time-consuming duties. She has a definite flair for free-lance writing using adequate vocabulary to express herself with clarity.

"The Faust family always attended the concerts," she said. Betty remembers when she was selected by Helena Mayor Thad Kelly in the fall of 1978 to serve on the Warfield Committee. "I was delighted to become a part of the most worthwhile endeavor I've ever had. It changed and broadened my life."

A few months later, she and Tom gaily entertained with a formal reception at their home to honor Metropolitan Opera singer, Gilda Cruz Roma, after her recital on March 3, 1979. Gilda is a gifted lyric soprano, retired now and teaching in San Antonio, Texas. We have continued to hear from each other through Christmas card correspondence.

Betty and I have shared some unusual situations. I once forced her into double duty before she had become accustomed to Warfield crises by calling for her to come to the Intensive Care Unit of the Helena Regional Medical Center when I was confined there with my heart attack. Later she told me how frightening she found the ICU, but bravely Betty came. I unloaded all my unfinished Warfield business on her and with her characteristic speed, everything was attended to and running smoothly.

Appointed by the Reverend Duane Saba in January 1991, Bettye Hendrix is the youngest of the three present Warfield Committee members. "Thrilled beyond words," she said, "when the call came telling of my appointment. Shocked and scared but I have given it my best and have found my efforts very rewarding."

Her fashionably cut black hair, dark eyes, and fair complexion respond to bright colors. Among her favorites are purple, crimson, and thalo green. Her neat appearance and eyes that express composure are the outward and visible signs of a nature filled with dependability and organized living.

Like an English nobleman with the Privy Purse, Bettye is the keeper of Warfield finances. She makes reports, pays the artists and other constantly emerging bills. She manages donations, oversees all records and files, and writes notes to acknowledge memorials. She is a valuable and vital part of the Warfield Committee.

Cassie Brothers is in her fifteenth year on the committee. In a way that is a long time, but it takes three or four years of service to sufficiently absorb the needed ability to make good judgments.

Her position represents Temple Beth El. She was appointed by Rabbi James Wax. Cassie thinks, "Warfield Concerts are the best thing going for the community, and I am grateful to be included in it.

Trying to please everyone is the hardest part of the work and we are overjoyed when people like our choices."

She has recently retired from her position as Library Supervisor for the Helena-West Helena School District. Having a masters degree in library science, she was on the Arkansas Library Commission and president of the Arkansas Library Association.

In all her undertakings, her husband, Bill, is ever-supportive. Bill has retired from the Board of Visitors of Phillips Community College of the University of Arkansas. Together, they are an admirable force in the education process of Phillips County.

For Warfield Concerts, Cassie and Bill have given numerous receptions honoring the artists. Out-of-town guests also enjoy their warm hospitality. They have a special way of making their company feel completely at home.

If housing is needed for performers, the Brothers' home is one of the first to be used. With no way of entering Helena except in a private car, Bill has gladly made runs back and forth to the Memphis Airport to accommodate the comings and goings of performers.

Cassie and Bill have acquaintances in other parts of the state. They have been influential in encouraging them to attend the concerts.

Working on the Warfield Committee with the two Bettys and Cassie has been most agreeable. We have learned from each other as we shared our duties and

obligations and developed friendships. We have floated on air with successes or consoled each other in dis-
appointments. If our opinions have differed, we have
tried to understand the opposite view or maybe compromise. Such are the relationships of true friends.

Now in my retirement, we are often in touch with
one another, and I continue to feel that they are and
forever will be my true friends.

Sine Finem

In four more fading summer days, I will be 88, Oct. 1, 1997. The calendar denotes the fall season, but here in the Mississippi Delta warm weather lingers. We are forced to wear light clothing for comfort. Every morning, I look expectantly at my indoor-outdoor thermometer, for a lower temperature reading. Thus far no significant change has appeared. Outside nature is flourishing: the marigolds, geraniums, and hibiscus adore the autumnal sunshine. Even the grass is thriving and soon will be in need of another cutting.

At eighty-eight, I can understand why older people like to reminisce. My thoughts comprise a mountain of memories, and I enjoy recounting stories of bygone days. Perhaps my remembering is the reason I have been able to write about S.D. Warfield and his legacy for free concerts.

Whenever the question is asked, "Why did you decide to write a book?" My answer is detailed and long.

During many Sunday afternoon visits with Miss Lily Peter at her modest little home in the countryside twelve miles south of Marvell, Arkansas, I told her the most recent news about Warfield Concerts. We laughed over the artists, what they said and what they liked and did not like. She was amused when hearing of exceptional situations that sometimes occurred during concerts. Then ladylike Miss Lily in her gentle manner would say, "These stories need to go in a book. My dear, please write about them."

Miss Lily was a Doctor of Philosophy and an author and poet for whom I had infinite respect. This brilliant lady lived to be one hundred with a perfectly clear mind. Many people remember her best as the Poet Laureate of Arkansas, but I will perhaps remember her best as a great friend and an inspiration.

Still, I did not take seriously what she said, not even giving it a second thought. I could not imagine myself undertaking the writing of a readable book.

My education in composition or theme writing has been limited to high school English under Mrs. May M. Brown, whose superb teaching skills left indelible impressions on generations of students. She strongly believed in memorizing quotations from Shakespearean plays. We were made to stand and recite them in front of everyone in the class. She drilled us on those from *Hamlet*. I can easily recall the last two lines of Polunuis's advice to his son, Laertes. "This above all: To thine own self be true, and it must follow as the night the day. Thou canst not then be false to any man."

In Mrs. Brown's classroom, across the top of the blackboard in twelve inch tall Old English script were the words: "Not For School But For Life We Learn." I have had a lifelong benefit from being in her classes, and feel a deep gratitude toward her.

A compelling force to make me finally pick up a pen and start writing came from my dear friend of many years, Mr. James Pelham "Doc" Baker. A graduate of Washington and Lee University School of Law, he has practiced law in Helena and West Helena for over fifty years. During that time, he was state senator for twelve years. A devoted member of St. John's Episcopal Church, Mr. Baker was once senior warden for three consecutive years.

His love of music plus his lifelong friendship with S.D. Warfield has given him a deep interest in the free Warfield Concerts. Doc remembers S.D.'s regular visits in the Baker home on Saturday afternoon to listen to the Texaco radio broadcasts of the Metropolitan Opera. Often S.D. became enthralled beyond reality with the music and would stand in front of the radio waving his hands as he pretended to be the conductor. To support him in his attempted impersonation, others in the room gave him lively applause.

Doc was in accordance with Miss Lily that a book should be written about the concerts, and he thought I ought to be the one to do it. That did not happen overnight but, after talking with him and his wife, Sara, in time, I did get started.

My lawyer friend was persistent in his encouragement, giving me confidence by saying, "Your inimitable tenacity will carry you through." Bulldogged tenacity may not always be appropriate, but in my case intense perseverance has been necessary to reach what I now think is time to stop writing.

Three different people have been my typists. My grandson Clopton Wolf, a senior in high school, gave many of his free hours to typewrite the first part of the story. Pat Brocato who is employed by the Helena-West Helena School District came to my rescue with her electric typewriter. She said she enjoyed reading my hand-written pages. I am most appreciative for her invaluable help. Good fortune arrived, when I found Sharon Kemp Crumby and her infallible computer. Sharon is an Office Technology Instructor at our local Phillips College. She takes my scribbled writing and brings back beautiful and meticulously done pages of double spaced flawless keyboarding presented in labeled folders. If more copies are needed, the computer zips them out. Sharon, please accept my heartfelt thanks. To all three of these willing typists, I offer my gratitude.

Unlike old-fashioned stories ending with the leading characters living happily evermore, or tragedies concluding when the principals are killed, or a mystery that divulges a plot, I do not have a normal stopping point for the book. It is a true recital about real people and real happenings that exist or have existed.

After changing my mind several times about a title, the final decision is *Free Tickets* because the unique quality of these high-class Warfield Concerts is the fact that they are free.

As far as anyone knows, there will be Warfield Concerts into perpetuity. The end of October 1997 brings the Moscow Boys Choir and in December, a Christmas Concert. In the spring of 1998, the famous New York City Opera National Company will stop here to present Donizetti's *Daughter of the Regiment*. Next season is already fully scheduled. As months and years unfold we will be blessed with delightful free concerts.

Having put my heart into Warfield Concerts for more than a quarter of a century, I wonder with genuine concern about the future. New laws may affect them. Inexperienced and uncaring committees or trust officers could blemish them. Even now, declining interest rates are making a decided mark on the amount of annual income for concerts. These conjectures are not intended to be alarming and are just passing thoughts with no idea of disturbing a soul.

Far better than negative reflections is a true message I hereby give to my readers: Whether a casual reader or a reader to be looking for historical facts, I hope this book will serve some purpose. Above all else, please enjoy and treasure the beautiful music we have had and will have through the amazing generosity of Samuel Drake Warfield.